# Cats, Mats and Marketing Plans

## How to build a simple marketing strategy and avoid complexity as your business grows

Roger Edwards

First printing: 2020

ISBN-13: 979-8686909212

British Cataloguing Publication Data:
A catalogue record of this book is available from
The British Library.

Also available for Kindle.

"There is a saying, often misattributed to Einstein, that everything must be made as simple as possible, but not one bit simpler. Roger has accomplished just that – he has provided a clear roadmap on how to avoid complexity and how to make your marketing strategy simple. Do your business a favour – read this book!"

**Vladimir Vulic, Montenegro**

*Digital transformation strategist. Co-founder of Digitalizuj.me. Programme Director of Spark.me conference. Keynote speaker in twenty countries across four continents.*

"From the outset, Roger sets the perfect tone for an unforgettable marketing know-how experience. From helping you figure out what needs to be fixed, through to the importance of keeping things simple to avoid complexity, this book serves it all up in a great bundle of business brilliance!"

**Chris Ducker, UK**

*Founder, Youpreneur.com and author of 'Virtual Freedom' and 'The Rise of the Youpreneur'*

"Man alive, the world needs this book! At a time when so much online noise makes it harder than ever to get your message across, we all need to understand true marketing like never before. Roger brings decades of practical experience to bear and a fierce passion to rid the world of jargon and bullshit and has produced a book of superb clarity and practicality. I learned loads and am already applying what I've learned to great effect!"

**Pete Matthew, UK**

*Host of the 'Meaningful Money' Podcast and author of 'The Meaningful Money Handbook'*

"Roger cuts through the marketing jargon and mumbo jumbo to bring us a highly practical guide to business marketing for the 2020s. This easy to follow and practical guide for anyone wanting to implement a marketing plan (or 'strategy', to use a bigger word than necessary) is both valuable and, delivered in Roger's inimitable style with many amusing anecdotes, a pleasure to read and absorb. If you want your small business to grow, build relationships with your customers and sell more, this is the guidance you need in a painless and entertaining manner."

**Paul McIntyre, UK**

*Coach, Mentor, Entrepreneurial Guide*

"Clarity is in short supply these days, despite being one of the most precious qualities of our media sphere. Roger has it in abundance. Marketing, that mysterious discipline full of buzzwords, myths, misconceptions, and fog, will never look so simple to you. As it should be. Marketing is, after all, deep down, just common sense of understanding who you are marketing to."

**Lazar Dzamic, Serbia**
*Co-author of 'The Definitive Guide to Strategic Content Marketing'*

"Our amazing digital world gives us so much choice in how we can market our businesses, but that doesn't mean we have to use everything! Roger is the undisputed master at keeping marketing simple, and his fantastic book proves that simple is best. If you want to spend more time on giving your customers an amazing experience and less time stressing over your marketing, this is the best book you'll ever read."

**Philip Calvert, UK**
*LinkedIn Expert and Keynote Speaker*

"Clever people make complex things simple. Fools make simple things complex. And when it comes to marketing, how do you learn to juggle cats and make it look simple? Roger Edwards is one of that very rare group of people who has been there and done it, right up to being CEO of a major FS company. He has worked with some of the best and brightest brains and now mentors, cajoles and influences today's and tomorrow's leaders too. It's a great track record but he's had his failures as well and he learns from failure every single time. If we're smart, we'll learn from his experiences and analysis, avoid the many pitfalls and – whisper it – start to enjoy the journey as well as the destination. Good heavens, this book even has cartoon zombies!"

**Andy Couchman, UK**
*Bankhouse Communications*

"Just like watching Roger on stage! He manages to perfectly transfer his stage energy into a book. Great read. Easy, simple and yet extremely useful and insightful. If you've watched Roger on stage, you'd enjoy this book. If you haven't already seen him on stage, you'd want to do that as soon as possible."

**Darko Buldioski, North Macedonia**
*Newmedia.mk and host of AllWeb Macedonia Conference*

"I run a small business and marketing has always felt to me like black magic. There seems to be a select few who 'know' and then there's the rest who must pay a fortune to get a slice of the knowledge. Not with this book though! Roger really digs deep into his personal (marketing) journey and after you've read the book, a lot of things become much clearer. I really like his down to earth approach and his denouncing of pointless corporate speak. Follow the steps outlined in his book and you will be much closer to understanding what to do in your business to achieve a much clearer marketing plan going forward."

**Nadin Thomson, UK**
*Lead at Business Image*

"Following a wobble in the clouds above the Alps, Roger was inspired to dispel the myth of marketing as a black art. He has reflected on what drives us to hit 'unsubscribe' more frequently these days, what we loved in the 80s about simple, easy to watch TV ads that we still remember with fondness today and how writing like we talk removes complexity. A thoroughly enjoyable and insightful read for everyone – not just budding marketers."

**Vicky Churcher, UK**
*Intermediary Director, AIG Life.*

"In this enthralling book, Roger Edwards has created not only a 'No BS' guide to marketing but also a value-packed handbook for anyone who wants to become (or is) a marketing pro. It's packed full of useful examples and tips as well as making excellent use of Roger's hallmark: brilliant storytelling. You will laugh out loud, cringe, gasp – maybe even need a stiff drink at times. But most of all, you will be educated and entertained by the bucket load. The perfect mix from this marketing maestro!"

**Eleanor Goold, Hungary**
*Founder, Kreativ Copywriting*

"Roger seriously gets it when it comes to marketing. Read this book to tap into his vast experience and transform your results. Roger's war against marketing complexity is a noble cause; your business and your customers will thank you for heeding his call to arms and joining the battle."

**Martin Bamford, UK**
*CEO of Bamford Media*

"Cats, Mats and Marketing Plans explains the core principles of marketing in a way that is accessible to those who just don't need the hyperbole and waffle of many books on marketing theory out there. Let's face it, there are plenty of people marketing businesses and products who don't have a degree and yet are at the coal face of delivering strategies to businesses. Edwards demonstrates the solid reasoning of keeping it simple, yet ensures marketers understand the importance of expanding the reader's knowledge from just delivering comms messaging. Intertwined with personal stories of campaigns delivered and arguments had, this is an easy read and a more direct route to marketing success."

**Paul Ince, UK**
*Founder of MarketedLive*

"This book by Roger Edwards fills a desperately needed gap in many unsuccessful online business person's skill sets, that of considering the areas of marketing that aren't the new sexy trends like live video or influencer marketing – the good old-fashioned idea of actually having some kind of consistent overall strategy in place. It also drives home the need for marketing to be part of the whole process of a business, all the way from initial product creation to delivery of the product to the customer. An essential resource for any serious small business owners in the new internet economy."

**Tim Lewis, UK**
*Stoneham Press*

For my wonderful wife, Trisha; our son Andrew, who has made us both so proud; and our cats: Lotty, who sits on our mat, and Jek and Sid, who now sit on stars and watch over us all.

# Foreword

I've had the pleasure of knowing Roger as a client, friend and work colleague for many years. We've worked together on many projects and shared stages at conferences around the world. I know how passionately he feels about marketing.

This book is a distillation of a career in marketing and a visceral reaction to the gobbledegook that so alienated him as he made his way through the conventional channels that tried to introduce him to the subject.

The first time I met Roger he was addressing his company field force at an internal company briefing. I remember thinking, even before we had spoken, that he was someone who tailored his message perfectly to his audience – a great and very necessary quality and one that he exhibits continually throughout this book.

I've discussed a lot of this stuff with Roger whilst enjoying a beer or two over the years and have experienced similar frustrations for similar reasons. The structure and process of business life, along with the strangleholds that the big consultancies have on our thinking, prevents us from doing what he has done, which is to challenge and adapt his own ideas. He's never let his focus on the customer and simplicity be worn down by corporate institutions that thrive on complexity.

What emerges from this experience is a very readable, deeply practical book with a strong emphasis on understanding and valuing customers in a way that so many companies in the financial services industry, where Roger and I have spent our working lives, are so often unable to do.

The construction of an 'Offer–Goal–Activity' model is logically and entertainingly explained, and Roger is not afraid to debunk conventional wisdom based on his personal exposure to some very practical challenges during his time in corporate life.

I really enjoyed the book and found it extremely easy to get into. It's very readable throughout but didn't develop in the way I expected. I had thought it was going to be the sort of book I used to buy at the airport to read on a flight to Dublin or Zurich.

But it's more heavyweight than that – justifiably and entertainingly heavyweight. Every section is well-crafted and argued but it is not a long read by marketing textbook standards. I like the practical diversions into Roger's own experience that make it real and explain why he thinks what he thinks.

So, despite his strong emphasis on simplicity, this is also a book with depth and robust argument. And it is also fun. Someone wanting to understand marketing, really understand it, could not do better than spend an afternoon delving into this very enjoyable and educational read.

**Peter LeBeau, MBE**
*MD of LeBeau Visage and Co-chair of Protection Review*

# Contents

# Introduction, and who this book is for

*What if the audience thinks my messages are too simple?*

This thought came rushing into my mind as I sat on an aeroplane, 35,000 feet above the Alps. Beyond the oval window I could see clear blue sky, snow-tipped mountains and lakes glistening in the sunlight. Sipping my free orange juice, I tried to clear this question from my thoughts and get back to running through the speech I would give in a couple of days' time.

*If everything goes to plan, I'll run onto the stage to techno dance music: a pounding beat, the swirling melody of a synth. With my right foot forward, I'll punch the air with my right hand – a good hard jab to an imaginary opponent's jaw – followed by a left cross and another knockout right jab. Switching to left foot forward, I'll attack again with a left jab, right cross and left hook.*

*Then, with a pre-agreed signal to the audio-visual guys, the music will cut out and I'll start my speech.*

*Complexity. Bureaucracy. Bloat. Management-speak mumbo jumbo. And just plain idiocy.*

*These are the enemies of effective customer-focused marketing. Whether your company is small, growing or a big corporate, these enemies can creep up on you. Infiltrate you.*

*Today we're going to fight back against complexity.*

*Are you up for a fight?*

*If the audience reply to my question and I sense they're game, I'll try to get an even louder response.*

*I said, "Are you up for a FIGHT?"*

*Hopefully 200 people will shout back, "YES!"*

I smiled at this image and for a moment I feel elated. But then the nagging little voice of doubt raises itself again.

*What if the audience thinks my messages are too simple?*

If only Montenegro Airlines gave out wine or beer as well as free soft drinks. I felt like I needed something a little stronger.

I was on my way to a marketing conference in Podgorica to give a speech called *Fighting Complexity in Marketing*. The organisers invited me because they had seen a video of my performance at CMA Live, an earlier conference in Edinburgh.

Edinburgh went well. At that point it was perhaps the most important speech of my entire 25-year marketing career, containing so many ideas and stories about keeping marketing simple, which I'd collected and filed away in my anecdote drawer while working in companies small, medium and large. The Edinburgh audience lapped up my material, responded loudly to my questions and took part in my examples.

They loved my *cat sat on the mat* story, which has since become my signature presentation segment (and which gave me the inspiration for this book and its title).

So, I should have been feeling confident, motivated and ready to rock the Montenegro stage. Instead, I felt a sinking feeling and a rush of nerves.

Pushing a trolley between them, the cabin crew made another pass up the aisle. I asked for a black coffee instead of another orange juice. As the attendant handed me the hot paper cup, the self-doubt began again.

*What the hell are you doing? In two days, you're going to be on a stage in front of an audience of 200 people for whom English is not their first language. And they're marketing directors of big companies, or marketing agency people. Can you really teach them anything? Will they be remotely interested in keeping things simple?*

I wondered what the odds were the plane would develop a technical fault and we'd divert to Austria.

What was wrong with me? What was the problem? Why was I suffering from imposter syndrome right now?

The Edinburgh audience were also marketing directors of big companies or marketing agency people. And lots of small business owners and entrepreneurs, too. They enjoyed my talk and took copious notes. They tweeted out positive comments. One delegate even made fancy drawings on artwork paper to go with her notes (they're called sketchnotes, I believe). She later sent me Polaroids of them, along with a thank you.

I had sturdy material. Perhaps the language barrier was generating my anxiety? Or the fact I wouldn't know anyone in either the audience or the conference team? In Edinburgh I knew the conference organisers and quite a few people in the audience, too. They were friendly, reassuring and supportive faces.

The reality was that I was experiencing classic imposter syndrome: the inability to acknowledge my own accomplishments and an ongoing fear of someone exposing me as a fraud. I was doubting my own abilities despite a strong track record.

Giving myself a virtual kick up the backside and drinking down a slug of hot, strong, black airline coffee, I dragged my thoughts back to running through the speech.

The captain announced 15 minutes to landing. Time to focus.

The stunning views on the approach into Podgorica side-tracked my thoughts again. After flying over Dubrovnik in Croatia, we descended over mountains into Montenegro. Podgorica nestles in a flat area of land surrounded by mountains. The plane flew over the city and swept around Skadar Lake to the south to line up for final approach.

Despite my worries, everything turned out fine.

Andrijana, a member of the conference organiser's team, met me at the airport, and over the next few days she and the team made me feel so welcome. She took me to the hotel, checked me in, and later collected me and the other speakers for dinner and wine tasting with the team in a restaurant on the shores of Skadar Lake.

By the time I took to the stage to the sounds of the pounding techno music two days later, I felt I knew the conference team well, and I'd already had many great conversations with the other guests.

The audience loved the speech.

I'd adapted it, of course, to compensate for the language difference. In the version of the talk I gave in Edinburgh and other UK cities earlier in the year, I'd used the word *muppetry* in the opening instead of *idiocy*. *Muppetry* is one of my favourite made-up words; it encapsulates the bureaucracy and stupidity some companies show in their marketing. But the audience in Montenegro wouldn't know what *muppetry* meant in the context of big companies doing stupid things.

But other than a few similar minor changes, it was the same *Fighting Complexity in Marketing* speech I'd done in Edinburgh and many times since.

And guess what?

They applauded the simple messages. They loved the *cat sat on the mat* segment. They wanted to talk afterwards about how simple marketing could be and, perhaps more importantly, how simple marketing strategy could be.

My fear that the audience would think my messages were too simple was unfounded. They positively embraced the simplicity – they were crying out for it. Afterwards, I was somewhat embarrassed but humbled that some of the guests wanted to take selfies with me.

That's when I realised I had to write this book.

Because companies the world over make marketing, especially the strategy part, far too complicated. Marketing is vital for business success and yet people starting businesses and trying to get to grips with it find it overwhelming.

If you haven't done a course at college or a degree at university, or worked in a marketing department, trying to learn the basics can be bewildering. There's so much on the internet about marketing that it's difficult to know where to start.

You'll find hundreds of thousands of articles, online courses, e-books and books (the irony of me adding another one to the list isn't lost on me!). There are degrees and MBAs, and we've created a whole language, jargon and mythology reinforced by all these authors, academics and practitioners.

You'll hear talk of SWOT analysis. PEST analysis. Boston Grids. Ansoff's matrices. Maslow's Hierarchy of Needs. You'll find models such as the STP (Segment – Target – Position). You'll learn about the 4Ps of marketing. Or is it the 7Ps of marketing? Or even the 11Ps of marketing! It can be all of them.

Some talk about strategy when they mean tactics. Others talk about marketing purely as a discipline of communication. And as a result, many people see marketing as synonymous with advertising and promotion. It isn't simple and it isn't engaging. It's just about communications, or more likely spam email and intrusive bombardment of annoying messages.

My aim with this book is to make marketing simple. And, most importantly, to make marketing strategy simple.

Marketing is so much more than advertising and promotion. We must think about the customer – what they need and how our products and services can help them – before we ever put pen to paper, or type words on a screen, or press send on an email, or sign off an advertising campaign.

You *must* have a strategy.

But strategy is a word people associate with complexity and painful, long awaydays locked in meeting rooms with piles of Post-it notes and marker pens.

Young people shy away from strategy because the way some companies do it sucks the energy and creativity out of them. The veterans resign themselves to it because they lack the will to fight against the way some companies do it: strategy sucked the energy and creativity out of them long ago.

In this book I'll show you how to put together a simple marketing strategy. We're aiming for simple. And we're aiming for engaging.

Who is this book for?

This book is for people running small businesses. People wanting to start small businesses. People who don't know much about marketing. Maybe people who think it's a black art. Or complicated, expensive and full of snake oil salesmen.

I want everyone to understand what marketing is. The full process, not just the bit we call communications. Or digital marketing, or social media marketing.

My aim is to teach you about marketing without getting complicated or using jargon, management-speak mumbo jumbo and gobbledegook. To avoid the word strategy as much as possible but still allow you to put one together using a simple method.

Maybe after reading this book, you'd like to explore a bit more of the traditional discipline and, dare I say, the more academic stuff.

While I'd love everyone to read it, this book isn't going to do much for people with marketing degrees, marketing MBAs or people high up in big corporate marketing roles. You're likely to find it too simplistic – basic, even. And you'll probably disagree with many of the things I say. But if you do read it then I'd love your feedback. My heart's in the right place, after all, and I'd be delighted if I made you question any complexity in your environment.

After the little wobble in the clouds above the Alps, the Montenegro conference made me confident people won't think my messages are too simple. I then knew I wanted to get something out there and help others find the simplicity they crave.

Can I really teach them anything? *Yes.*

Will they be remotely interested in keeping things simple? *Damn right!*

The book you're holding is the result.

# Part one:
# About marketing and why, in some areas, it needs fixing

# Is marketing broken and can we fix it?

Marketing is broken! Busted. Smashed. Kaput.

Except when it's done with integrity, and a deep, almost obsessive understanding of the customer.

You can see it's broken in many brands and companies. It's a tsunami of badly targeted emails, social media broadcasts, intrusive adverts, annoying video pop-ups and cold calls. With big corporates, it can be a mass of complexity, bloat, management-speak mumbo jumbo and jargon. It's marketing that doesn't engage the customer; it enrages them.

With integrity and a deep, almost obsessive understanding of the customer we can fix broken marketing. By reading this book I hope you'll feel inspired to play your part when marketing your own business.

But first we need to understand why it's broken.

## It's not all about communications

I think there are three reasons, and the first is what marketing means to most people. Ask someone on the street or in a coffee shop and they'll say one of the following: advertising, promotion, commercials, emails or social media. These are all good answers because they are all part of marketing. But marketing is so much more than this.

Marketing just means communications to so many people these days, even those who do marketing for a living.

If you look at the traditional discipline of marketing, by reviewing the syllabus of a marketing MBA for example, it includes customer orientation, research, segmentation, targeting, positioning, strategy, product, price, distribution, communications, people and brand.

Communications is only a small part of what marketing is all about, but it's often all we hear about.

The long-term outcome of this trend is that marketing has become the department or people who just do the communications, or the *colouring-in department*, as I've heard people describe it. And we've created a whole generation of marketers who don't do research and so don't have that deep understanding of their customer – they just send out endless waves of communications.

## It can be intrusive and annoying

The second problem is marketing can be intrusive and annoying. When was the last time you hit the unsubscribe link on an email? I'd guess most of us will have clicked on such a link, perhaps with a big sigh or frustrated grunt, within the last few days. Why did you hit unsubscribe? The chances are the emails had started to annoy you.

I often subscribe to email lists simply to check out the content, style, headlines and messages they use to see what I can learn. I once jumped on the list of a famous American copywriter and one day I received an invitation to his latest webinar.

The headline was something like *Sign up to my webinar to find out how to earn a million bucks in less than a week without doing any work.* As the day of the webinar fast approached, he upped the number of emails advertising his event: *Only five days left to sign up to my webinar to find out how to earn a million bucks in less than a week without doing any work.*

Daily emails, sometimes twice daily, popped into my inbox. On the day of the webinar I went to bed (there was an eight-hour time difference between the UK and the part of the US where this guy was based) and woke the next day to six emails from him.

*Only six hours left to sign up to my webinar to find out how to earn a million bucks in less than a week without doing any work.* Then *Only five hours left to sign up to my webinar ...* Then *Only four hours left ...* You get the picture.

I finally hit the unsubscribe button. It's a shame it only took a mouse click to excuse myself from his list. I'd have preferred a giant red button I could have brought my fist down on with a satisfying thump.

Other marketing communications have us bubbling with anger too, such as those unsolicited telephone calls trying to sell us wall insulation, and ambulance-chasing lawyers who gleefully tell us we've been in a car accident and can get compensation, even though we haven't, and we can't.

Then there's TV advertising. There's nothing worse than getting stuck into an episode of *Games of Thrones, Downton Abbey* or *Love Island,* only for the ad break to interrupt us just as it's getting juicy. If you're like me you probably record your programmes in advance, or at least watch them on timeslip 15 minutes ahead, so you can fast forward through the adverts. That's our big red button for avoiding them.

What about pop-up ads on your computer or mobile device? There's a big red button called a pop-up blocker for that.

Wherever enraging marketing exists there's usually a big red button to stop it. But here's something to think about. If we don't like these marketing tactics as individuals and customers, why would we as business owners or marketers feel it's okay to do it to others?

Surely it's better to engage with your customer rather than enrage them?

## It can be complex

The third problem with marketing is products, services and communications are often complex, especially from big corporates, with difficult-to-understand products and tortuous customer-service processes complicated by unreadable language. Blighted by passive sentences, long words and jargon, it's gobbledegook, codswallop, poppycock, balderdash. It's just bollocks.

As we work through the book, I'd like to help you avoid these three danger zones.

You can solve problem number one by understanding marketing is not just about communications. It's about research: understanding customer needs, putting together an offer in the form of a simple product or service and then looking to the communications.

You can solve problem two by putting together engaging communications that don't intrude or annoy; communications your customers might want to consume.

And you can solve problem three by fighting back against complexity. That means simple products, simple service and simple marketing communications.

Customers dislike complexity; they recoil from it. Give them something simple and they'll love it – but keeping things simple is hard. It needs commitment, focus and consistency. The fact that simple is harder to do is the reason so many things are complicated.

Businesses might start out with the best intentions, but as companies become successful and grow, complexity starts to infiltrate like silent assassins slipping in under the cover of night. Complex enrages customers. Simple engages them. Who's more likely to buy? The enraged or the engaged?

Engage. Don't enrage.

Let's start by going right back to basics.

# What is marketing?

What is marketing? The answer isn't as easy as you might think.

Look on Google, listen to people with marketing qualifications or who work in marketing departments, talk to academics and listen to the opinions of people who've never been near a marketing department in their lives. You'll find thousands, if not millions, of answers.

Those answers will have common features, but you won't find one definitive definition. Or at least not one everyone agrees on. The truth is it's hard to put into a few words a massive discipline developed over decades. A discipline taught in universities and business schools all over the world. With many professional organisations committed to its practice and development. About which experts have written countless books, and which drives hundreds, if not thousands, of conferences each year.

A discipline now changing on a daily, if not hourly, basis as we invent new digital methods of communication, data collection, storage, analysis and research.

Each university and each business school has a slightly different definition of marketing. Each professional organisation has an alternative take on a key element of marketing. One author will word things differently to another and each conference presenter will put their own spin on the subject.

The Harvard Business School defines marketing as follows:

*Marketing helps a firm in creating value by better understanding the needs of its customers and providing them with innovative products and services. This value is communicated through a variety of channels as well as through the firm's branding strategy. Effective management of customers and pricing allows the firm to capture part of the value it has created. Finally, by building an effective customer-centric organisation, a firm attempts to sustain value over time.[1]*

It's a bit wordy, but I like this robust definition. The important part to zoom in on is *understanding the needs of its customers.*

The Chartered Institute of Marketing in the UK describes marketing as:

*The management process for identifying, anticipating and satisfying customer requirements profitably.[2]*

This glorious and simple definition notes the need to meet customer needs but also to make profit. Unless you are a charity, we're all in business to make money.

The equivalent professional body in the US, the American Marketing Association, says:

*Marketing is the activity, set of institutions, and processes for creating, communicating, delivering, and exchanging offerings that have value for customers, clients, partners, and society at large.[3]*

For me, this doesn't talk about customer needs enough.

I like Dr Philip Kotler's definition:

*The science and art of exploring, creating, and delivering value to satisfy the needs of a target market at a profit.*

*Marketing identifies unfulfilled needs and desires. It defines, measures and quantifies the size of the identified market and the profit potential. It pinpoints which segments the company is capable of serving best and it designs and promotes the appropriate products and services.[4]*

---

1 https://www.hbs.edu/faculty/units/marketing/Pages/default.aspx (accessed January 2020)

2 https://www.cim.co.uk/qualifications/get-into-marketing/ (accessed Jan 2020)

3 https://www.ama.org/the-definition-of-marketing-what-is-marketing/ (accessed Jan 2020)

4 https://www.kotlermarketing.com/phil_questions.shtml#answer3 (accessed Jan 2020)

Kotler keeps the simplicity of the CIM definition while nudging us a little more on the actions we have to take.

What about marketing practitioners? Professionals at the coalface and in boardrooms? I've come across some great definitions from corporate marketers.

Steve Dickstein, chief executive officer at Hugo Naturals, says:

*Marketing is delighting a consumer, customer and/or user to achieve a profit or other pre-established goal.*[5]

I love the phrase, *delighting a customer*!

Paul Kulavis, managing partner at Sterling Park Group, says:

*Marketing is discovering what the prospect wants and demands and delivering it more efficiently and effectively than the competition.* [5]

This definition, unlike the others we've seen so far, introduces the need to be better than our competitors.

Mary Ellen Bianco of Getzler Henrich & Associates LLC says:

*Marketing includes research, targeting, communications and often public relations. Marketing is to sales as ploughing is to planting for a farmer – it prepares an audience to receive a direct sales pitch.* [5]

Mary's definition is great because she recognises the crucial relationship between sales and marketing.

Beyond corporates, here are a few definitions from *celebrity* marketing experts you see regularly on stages at marketing conferences around the world.

Joe Pulizzi says:

*Marketing is identifying the pain points of your customers,*

5 https://heidicohen.com/marketing-definition/ (accessed Jan 2020)

*developing content and processes to best solve those pain points –*
*which ultimately makes it easier for your customers to buy or stay*
*customers.*[5]

Pain points are simply a more dramatic way of saying *needs*. But sometimes dramatic helps to put the idea across better.

Mark Schaefer says:

*Marketing is influencing behaviour to get more people to buy more*
*stuff, more often, for more money.*[5]

Once you look beyond those in academia, people in marketing jobs and experts, and go out and ask random people on the street what marketing is, I think most would say *advertising and promotion.*

And while it's true that advertising and promotion are important parts of the marketing discipline, it's much more than just advertising and promotion. Marketing involves research, but it's much more than just research. Marketing involves building products and services, but it's much more than just building products and services.

It's no wonder it can appear bewildering to newcomers or as a black art to the uninitiated.

One thing's for sure though. No matter what your definition of marketing, or which university, business school, professional organisation, book or conference it came from, marketing is one of, if not *the* most important activity a company of any size should undertake.

And it all starts with the customer.

I don't have a one-line definition of marketing. In this book I'm going to give you a simple model, the Offer–Goal–Activity model. And it starts with an important statement.

*Marketing is a deep, almost obsessive understanding of our*
*customers.*

Marketing defines who our customers are, and our deep understanding of those customers means we can then:

- find out what our customers need
- work out which products and services we need to make to meet those needs
- decide how much to charge for our products and services so we can make a profit
- decide where and how we're going to sell them
- put together the branding, packaging and customer experience
- plan what advertising, promotion and content we must create to communicate with those customers about how our products or services meet their needs.

That's why I decided, for the purposes of this book, not to try to come up with another all-embracing definition of marketing. We don't need another one.

What I hope to do is:

First, convince you that marketing starts with the customer. Always.

Second, show you that marketing is so much more than just communications.

Third, give you an uncomplicated way of putting together a simple marketing strategy. That's the Offer–Goal–Activity model.

Finally, help you keep things simple, no matter how big or successful you become. Show you how to keep complexity, bureaucracy, bloat, mumbo jumbo and bullshit at bay as you keep marketing your products and services, keep growing your sales and keep growing your business.

# Getting started in marketing – a personal account

We are the sum of our experiences. We learn from everything we do in life: every mistake we make, every success we celebrate. And I'm still learning every day. I know a good amount about marketing, but I never call myself an expert. Or a *guru.*

The world is changing so quickly that I don't think anyone can claim to be an expert – we're all genuinely learning and reassessing the craft day by day. But sometimes it's good to look back at some of your experiences and reflect on how they shaped your current skills, knowledge and view of the world.

Some of my earliest memories of marketing are from when I was at school. Our English teacher, Steve Plowes, was eccentric and had a glittering personality. With wild arm gestures, a wide vocal range and a powerful presence, he resembled a one-man theatre company.

Mr Plowes spent hours reading books aloud to us. He treated each book as a theatrical performance and would include nonfiction books in his repertoire.

One day, sweeping into class with his battered leather satchel, he held up a new book with a burgundy hardback cover, which was all about advertising. He started to read, adding his theatrical flourishes to the story of real advertising experts.

Hearing about the methods they used to try to encourage people to buy their stuff fascinated me. I rarely went home and raved to my parents about the books we read, but I went on at them about this *adverts* book.

As an older schoolboy I took A Level economics and part of the syllabus was about marketing. What attracted my interest most was something called *The Product Lifecycle.*

As we learned about the four phases of the product lifecycle, that was the moment I became truly hooked on marketing.

- *Introduction:* researching, developing and then launching the product.
- *Growth:* when product sales are increasing at their fastest rate.
- *Maturity:* when sales are their highest but flattening out. The rate of growth is slowing because new competitors come into the market, the market is saturated, or your product is going out of fashion.
- *Decline:* the final stage of the cycle, when sales begin to fall.

The teacher explained how to extend the product lifecycle to make it last longer. For example, they could take steps to stop it going into decline with a kick starter advertising campaign.

I found it fascinating and fun. And, unlike subjects such as history and geography, I could see a definite real-world application. Economics fuelled my interest in marketing, and I started looking for examples of excellent product development and attractive advertising.

Back then, in the early 1980s, we only had four channels on the TV to choose from: BBC One, BBC Two, Independent Television (ITV) and the newly launched Channel 4. ITV and Channel 4 funded their programming through advertising. So, while my mum and dad dived into the kitchen to make a cup of tea or grab a cheeky whisky during the commercial breaks, I'd stay and watch the ads.

I remember so many great adverts from that era. Sometimes I look for them on YouTube and feel a shiver of nostalgia for family evenings in front of the telly.

My favourite advert was for a variety of instant mashed potato called Smash. Imagine colourful Martian robots in a spaceship talking, in Dalek-like voices, about how humans make mashed potato. The strapline, set to music, was the joyously simple *For mash get Smash.*

Other adverts I remember include: Cadbury's Flake – *Only the crumbliest, flakiest chocolate. Tastes like chocolate never tasted before.* And the Heineken beer commercials – *Refreshes the parts other beers cannot reach.*

As I watched the ads, I tried applying the lessons we'd learned in class. We were at the point in the syllabus that talked about a classic advertising formula called *AIDA*, which stands for:

- Attract
- Interest
- Desire
- Action

Smash, Cadbury's Flake and Heineken followed this formula. They attracted people's attention, stimulated their interest, created desire and prompted an action, in these examples to buy the instant mashed potato, chocolate or beer.

I went on to study economics at university and selected marketing as a subsidiary subject and it involved a much deeper dive into research, the product lifecycle, pricing and advertising. We learned about other advertising formulas as well as *AIDA*. Marketing was the most interesting part of my degree. Looking back, I can't remember why I didn't take a straight marketing degree. Maybe Leeds didn't offer one. Or maybe I liked the comfort blanket of my strongest school subject.

University wasn't just study, it was fun too: a blur of alcohol; my first serious, and not so serious, girlfriends; countless concerts; and an unsuccessful campaign to get myself chosen as the publicity secretary for the Progressive Rock Society. And while all these experiences flew by, a desire took a firm grip in my head. Marketing was the career I ultimately wanted to go into.

In the third year of university, studying for our final exams, we started approaching companies to line up a job after graduation. Sometimes the bigger corporates came to the university campus to carry out interviews.

My tactic was to start applying for marketing jobs in financial services and fast-moving consumer goods companies. I lined up a few interviews and realised I'd have to go and buy a suit. "Maybe I should have a haircut," I thought. My hair spilled down to my shoulders to reflect my love of heavy metal music.

The interviews went nowhere. They told me, "You aren't going to end up with the right qualification for a job in marketing. It's not because you don't have creative ideas. It's not because you don't come across well in your interview. Your marketing subsidiary subject counts for one sixth of the degree. The other five sixths are nothing to do with marketing. We want somebody who's thoroughly, utterly immersed in marketing, marketing strategy and marketing tactics. We're not looking for somebody who's only just scratched the surface."

But marketing was what I wanted to do. How could I get into it? One recruiter told me, "Well, it's a sort of Catch-22 situation, mate. You've not really got enough academic experience in marketing for a company to offer you a job. So, you need to get more experience. But the only way you can get experience is to go and work in a marketing role."

Together with my careers adviser we came up with a plan. I applied for various roles in companies with strong marketing departments, the idea being to learn about the company or industry and eventually work my way into the marketing department by building up some experience.

Leaving Leeds behind me, I found myself in the UK financial services industry with a summer job at an independent financial adviser firm in Bournemouth.

Sucking in knowledge every day, I learned how financial services works. But I had a keen eye on how they were promoting themselves, how they were developing products, how they were talking to their customers and how they were getting customers to buy their stuff.

The partners in the firm helped me to apply for jobs in big financial services companies, and towards the end of the summer several offers arrived at once. The one that appealed to me the most was a job in the technical support unit of a life insurance company. This department sat side by side with the marketing team, helping them come up with product specifications and writing the technical briefs for the product literature. The role sounded ideal and fitted the strategy I'd agreed with my university careers adviser. Here I could build the experience I needed to eventually make a well-timed jump into a marketing role. I accepted their offer and moved again, this time to the Lake District.

Starting with the new company, I had to learn the ropes from the bottom up. I made the coffee, photocopied and faxed. I sent the post out and managed the paper filing stack. Over the course of a couple of years I built myself a reputation as a great communicator inside the company and when corresponding with clients. As the technical services sat with marketing, we always got involved with product development. I saw the marketing process in real time for the first time. School and university presented the theory; here I could taste the practice. I saw research, product proposals, marketing communications plans, and I experienced the product launches. These were exciting times, but an opportunity to jump into marketing had yet to appear.

I also joined the company social club committee and helped them to organise events like Christmas parties, barbecues, pub quizzes, treasure hunts and sports competitions. And as part of the social club activity, I started using a skill I'd crafted while at school. Drawing cartoons.

Every month the company ran a raffle that most of the staff used to enter. One day we came up with the idea of doing cartoon entry forms for the raffle, using my drawings.

The raffle poster with my cartoon led to the breakthrough I needed. The marketing department was in full campaign mode, supporting the launch of a product to try to get people to save for future events, such as school fees planning for their children. The marketing manager went on a UK roadshow doing sales force training.

With the image of the marketing manager as a school head master in mind, for the next raffle entry form I flourished my ink pen and within minutes the marketing manager appeared on the paper, wearing an academic mortar board and black cloak, and wielding a cane.

After that raffle, my phone rang, and I heard the voice of the marketing manager. "I love the cartoon you drew of me for the raffle entry form, though I'm sure my nose isn't as big as all that! Roger, have you ever considered working in the marketing department?" I might have heard trumpets at that moment, or fireworks exploding. I do know I punched the air.

Suddenly I found myself in the marketing team doing everything from product development to market research and marketing communications. Over the next few years, I continued to build my knowledge and developed a reputation as a great communicator. I was out on the road with the sales force doing presentations, promoting the products and guiding the marketing communications.

My career in marketing had begun.

# Marketing isn't just about communications

Marketing isn't just about communications, but people without marketing experience think that's exactly what it is. Sadly, an increasing number of marketing people think that's all it is, too.

We hear about:
- Social media marketing
- Email marketing
- Influencer marketing
- Video marketing
- Blog marketing
- Digital marketing

It's the same at conferences. You'll see sessions with titles like:
- Social media marketing to maximise reach
- How video marketing can grow your sales
- Use email marketing to make profits

There's nothing wrong with these titles, nor the content. But what they're really describing here is communications, adverts, promotion and content.

Social media marketing is social media communication.

Email marketing is email communication.

Influencer marketing is really influencer communication.

Video marketing is video communication.

Blog marketing is really communication through blogging.

Digital marketing is online or app-based communications, as opposed to paper-based or traditional media, such as analogue television.

I talked earlier about going out onto the street and asking people what marketing is. Most would say advertising and promotion, but others might go further. Some might say spam email, cold calling or companies pestering you with pop-ups. Perhaps a few would say social media. Fewer would say content like blogs, podcasts and e-books. Communications, collectively, would be the most popular answer.

As a marketer with more than 25 years' experience, I know there's more to marketing than communications, much more.

Why? The lecturers drummed it into me at college. Managers kept banging on about it in my many junior marketing roles. And then, one day, I'd worked my way up the corporate ladder high enough to bang on about it to those working for me.

It took root during my first interview for a more senior marketing role. In the job description, the company explained the successful candidate would take responsibility for the *strategy and the marketing mix* for the product range.

The marketing mix.

Now that's not a phrase you hear much these days. If you go digging about you might still find it on university and business school syllabuses. Blow the dust off old marketing textbooks and you'll find it lurking inside. Where you won't hear it used much these days is in marketing departments themselves.

If the interview for the more senior role went well, taking the job on would mean a move to Edinburgh. I drove up from the north of England, passing through the gorgeous scenery of the Scottish Borders. Cobbled streets made the car shudder. I caught glimpses of the castle and Princes Street. Edinburgh looked like a wonderful place to visit. Would it make a good place to work? And live?

I met the marketing manager interviewing for the role. He asked me to explain my understanding of strategy and the marketing mix. I looked at him and something like this came out of my mouth.

*"Strategy is setting out the goal. Then planning to meet the goal by meeting a customer need. And the marketing mix is the tactics we use to fulfil the strategy to achieve the goal."*

The memory cheats. I bet I used much clunkier words and much more jargon, and I probably came out with a bit of gobbledegook. I probably used big words so he would think I was more impressive, hoping it may even encourage him to employ me. In fairness, this was many years before I developed my obsession with simplicity in marketing.

After I'd finished, he sat back and performed the gesture that I became very used to over the next few years. He made a steeple out of his fingers and rested his nose on the apex. My future manager seemed pleased with my articulation of a strategic goal and offer, and he urged me to explain the tactics available within the marketing mix.

Again, flicking through the textbooks still on a shelf in my head, I plucked out the 4Ps of marketing.

- The Product that meets the customer need
- The Price you charge for it
- The Place you sell it
- And what you do to Promote it

Place, of course, means distribution, or just sales. But I guess whoever invented the 4Ps had to call it something beginning with a P. Otherwise it wouldn't have been the 4Ps of marketing – it would have been the 3Ps and a D.

He must have liked my answers because he offered me the job. Exciting times, meaning my fiancée Trisha and me moving up to Edinburgh.

Once in the job, I learned a great deal from the marketing manager who made steeples out of his fingers. The need to balance strategy with tactics always featured on the agenda. Getting the strategy nailed before diving into the tactics was his constant refrain.

A stickler for research, Steeple Fingers wouldn't let me do anything without evidence to back up the decision. Even if we were putting together a simple one-page sales aid – effectively an advert on one side of a piece of paper – he'd want research. He was a stickler.

*"What's the goal for this sales aid? What is the call to action? What do you want people to do? Is it clear what our offer is?"*

Armed with answers to those questions, he'd want more. *"Research the words and the tone. Does it resonate with the audience? Does it help the sales guys explain the product? Does it make it easier for them to answer questions the customers are asking? Does it increase sales?"*

I found myself on the phone asking these questions of members of the sales team and the advisers they were talking to. For more substantial material, like a brochure or an advert that was going to appear in a magazine or on a billboard, he'd always start with the goal and the offer. Then we would take the drafts out to full research. This meant hiring people for a focus group.

Sitting behind a one-way mirror in a dedicated research suite, we'd watch and listen to their reactions to our product, copy or adverts. We'd use their feedback and opinions to shape our strategy, refine the offer and inform our tactics.

"We are always listening," Steeple Fingers told me. He taught me the difference between hearing and listening. "Lots of people *think* they're listening, but they're sitting there hearing a buzz. Their mind is elsewhere, thinking about what they want to say next. To listen you have to stop thinking of other things and concentrate on what the person is actually saying." And boy, did we listen. Research became key. We were always researching, and I know I'm a better marketer now because of it.

But as important as these lessons were, I did feel frustrated at first. I wanted to get stuck into the interesting stuff: drafting brochures, writing advertising copy, putting briefs together and liaising with agencies and creatives.

I wanted to sit in on agency pitch presentations and see all the creative boards they were holding up. I wanted to grin or wince at the headlines that didn't make their final recommendation, until finally they presented us with their preferred campaign – creative, distinctive, edgy and giving us the best chance to hit our goals.

To be honest, research was dull. Phoning people and talking them through a list of questions and all those focus groups gave us interesting insights, for sure, but they were often dull to listen to.

Steeple Fingers was a stickler but striving for balance between strategy and tactics paid off. We did the research, put the strategy in place and then got on with the tactics, and our company grew its market share. Massively.

From my studies I'd always known that, on paper, marketing wasn't just about communications, but here I was living it and breathing it and seeing it succeed. Twenty-five years later, I still understand the importance of putting strategy in place before tactics, but I hear so many companies talking about marketing now as if it's only about the tactics of communications.

Listening to the advice of some marketing experts and gurus, I can see why people do think it's just about communications. An expert will say we need to be on Twitter doing *Twitter marketing*. Another guru bounds onto a stage and screams we need to do *video marketing*. Others declare we need to be blogging. And in response, the marketing people within companies agree.

All these activities are perfectly good tactics in any marketing plan. Statistics back up their success.

But these gurus rarely talk about the research or understanding the customer enough to put together an offer that stands out.

They have superb communication skills and they can demonstrate huge success on Instagram and show off their hundreds of thousands of subscribers on YouTube or millions of followers on Twitter. The world's media hail them as marketing gurus, and conference organisers invite them onto stages in giant auditoriums. And while some have wider marketing pedigrees, others are solely experts in their chosen tactic of communication.

There's nothing wrong with this, of course. These experts work hard and deserve their success and their accolades. But they have also helped to shape the modern view marketing is just about the communications. We are in danger of forgetting about research, customer understanding, putting together offers and using the other tactical tools of product, price, place and promotion.

I can't be too critical. Thinking back to *young me*, I remember my eagerness to get to grips with writing brochures and ad copy and working with creative agencies, rather than being bored shitless doing telephone research or sitting behind those mirrors.

And today the communications toys are so much sexier: social media, apps, web platforms, email, bots, AI, VR and programmatic marketing. These shiny toys seduce all marketers, me included, and I still feel the seductive thrill when a new app tries to woo me into its embrace. No wonder everyone wants to play with the tactical toys. Who wants to bother with all the boring academic stuff?

Research? No thanks.

Goals? Uh huh.

Offers? *Please.*

The 4Ps? Nah, that's for naff old college professors.

I'm sorry though. As stuffy as it may seem, and as shiny as the toys have become, before you can dive into communications, promotions, advertising, social media engagement or whatever you want to call it, you must cover the other elements of the marketing discipline.

Before you can use tactics, you must have a strategy.

# Is strategy the problem with marketing strategy?

On stage at The Content Marketing Academy Live Conference in June 2017, I asked the audience a crucial question about their marketing.

CMA Live had been a regular event in Edinburgh since 2015 and brought in marketers and small business owners from all over the UK, Europe and beyond. In my opinion it was one of the best marketing events I've ever been to. I enjoyed being a delegate in 2016 and felt honoured when organiser Chris Marr asked me to give my *Fighting Complexity in Marketing* speech the following year. This was the first time I performed my now famous *cat sat on the mat* segment.

I strode on stage in front of 200 people at The Hub venue, an acoustically perfect old church with a vaulted ceiling, and asked the question, "By a show of hands, how many of you here today have a written marketing strategy?"

Only three people stuck up their hands. Three people out of two hundred. In fairness, many of them travelled to the conference to learn more about content marketing specifically and marketing in general, so I can forgive a sparse number of hands reaching for that gothic ceiling.

But three out of two hundred?

A few months later I hopped on a train down to Newcastle to deliver the same speech at a conference called Talking Point of Business. I asked the same question and got five out of sixty hands in response. A better percentage.

Four weeks later in Podgorica in the beautiful country of Montenegro, again to deliver the same speech. Again, I asked the same question. Six out of a hundred and fifty.

The same talk in Belgrade, Serbia in June 2018. Seven out of a hundred and fifty.

I've since delivered this speech in Romania, the Czech Republic, Albania and Macedonia, as well as many cities around the UK. On every occasion the number of people putting up their hands was around 5% of the audience.

So why did only 21 people out of 600 at the various conferences put their hands up and say they had a written marketing strategy? What's the problem with strategy? Why is something so important ignored by so many?

Over the last 20 years, in the small start-ups, medium-sized companies and big corporates I've worked for, strategy has a strange effect on people. Just the mention of the word can be enough to turn them off. Their eyes glaze over and they dive for cover, or they make an excuse to leave the room. Some talk of strategy with despair in their voices.

Would marketing be easier if we dumped the word *strategy*? If we removed it from the dictionary? Obliterated it from textbooks? Forbade its use at marketing conferences?

I think it would.

The word *strategy* stops people from being strategic. I think the *S-word* gets in the way of doing all the other parts of marketing.

What's the problem with the *S-word* then? Here are a few reasons why we'd be better off without it.

## It's a marketing buzzword

It's jargon. It's something the latest *entrepreneurs* on BBC's *The Apprentice* drop into every statement they make because they think Lord Sugar will be more impressed with their business acumen. It's as if talking strategy automatically makes people want to use big words, clichés and bombastic corporate language.

Put the word *strategic* in front of any other word and it makes it sound more corporate or academic, e.g. strategic review or strategic initiative.

Often it features in management-speak mumbo jumbo, for example, *our journey up the strategic staircase*. And when it's associated with management-speak it's hard to take seriously. Everyone laughs at management-speak behind its back, don't they?

It's hard to avoid jargon. I've been fighting against it for 20 years, but I still slip up and use it. I've probably missed some while writing this book. As marketers, we must talk in the language of our customers. Always.

## People associate it with complexity

Anyone who's ever worked in a big corporate will recognise, and dread, the annual strategic planning process.

That sinking feeling when the gigantic strategy pack holding hundreds of pages arrives with a thump on the desk. It even makes a resounding clang as it drops like a brick into your email inbox.

The heart sinks and shoulders slump. Everyone gets buckled in for two or three months of intense, repetitive dullness. Picture long awaydays and endless meetings with hours spent sticking Post-it notes on walls and then continually rearranging them until the notes lose their stickiness and flutter to the floor.

Senior management may bring in an external facilitator, perhaps a global consultancy brand. They'll have everyone doing *SWOT* analysis, which stands for *Strengths, Weaknesses, Opportunities and Threats*. Maybe *PEST* analysis, which stands for *Political, Economic, Social and Technological*. Also, *Ansoff's Matrix* and *Boston Grids*. If you're lucky they'll mention *Maslow's Hierarchy of Needs*.

This intellectualisation of marketing is often just a consequence of a company getting big. They can afford the six-figure consultants and need doctorate-level analysis paralysis to justify the price tag. The expensive consultants cloak strategy in mystique and create the impression it's only accessible to a few clever people. Some CEOs buy the argument and spend tons of money getting the six-figure consultants in to cut through this mystique.

The process can suck the life out of people. It can drain the creativity and motivation from even the most creative and motivated.

Many corporate people, therefore, associate strategy with a painful time in the business year. It's as if strategy comes with a health warning: *Beware. Horribly complex. Avoid at all costs.* Even if you don't work in a big company, there's enough complex material out there on the internet to convince people that strategy equals complex. The result? They shy away from it, and they don't do it.

## Many people confuse strategy with tactics

This is a symptom of the digital age. We all get excited by shiny new toys, whether it's a new app helping us tweet more effectively or a drone letting us film some drop dead gorgeous coastline shots for our vlogs. We want them, and we want them now.

Live streaming apps? *Yes please!*

New storytelling apps? *Yup, gimme.*

New ways of creating graphics? *Yep, sign me up.*

New ways of creating webpages? *Okay – stick me on the alert list.*

It's natural to want to play with the latest gizmos and use them to get our messages out there and engage with our customers. The problem is most of these apps and most of these platforms are tactical. And tactics don't work without a strategy.

And some *influencers* compound the problem. We see Instagram experts and Periscope and Twitter gurus who are doing so well in business that they lead jet-set lifestyles and get to speak in front of stadium-sized audiences. It might lead us to believe these tactics on their own are enough to build a business.

And as some of these influencers use the word *strategy* when they mean *tactics*, people believe tactics and strategies are the same. They aren't. You need a strategy to plan your tactics.

There's nothing wrong with their enthusiasm and advice for their speciality areas, but only the best influencers talk about their toys in the context of a proper business model.

# It doesn't fit with people's day-to-day work

Because it seems boring, complex, and academic, and people associate it with senior management disappearing off for a jolly to some country house for a few days, they don't see the connection to their day jobs.

Employees want to do a decent job and hit their targets. They want to build positive relationships with customers and colleagues and maybe even have some fun at the same time – where shall we go after work on Friday night?

Strategy is detached from this. It's aloof, unapproachable. Even the most passionate employees, those who want their company to succeed, don't see how strategy is going to help.

If marketing buzzwords, jargon and black magic terms create dread in people's minds, not to mention the complexity, perhaps it is indeed time to abandon the word *strategy* and all the guff associated with it.

Instead, make it easy and interesting. Fun, even.

How can we make sure businesspeople understand the simple steps they need to go through to market their business effectively? And can we talk them through those steps, on their terms and in their language?

I've wrestled with this during my years in big corporates and I believe we can make strategy simple and fun. The Offer–Goal–Activity model we'll get to later in this book gives you a framework for putting together a marketing strategy without actually using the word *strategy*.

But before we get to the simple model, let's have a look at why I became obsessed with keeping things simple.

# The start of my obsession with keeping marketing simple

Just as my old boss, Steeple Fingers, was a stickler for doing research, when I was the boss, my people saw me as a stickler for simplicity. I'd call people out on management-speak, jargon and mumbo jumbo. I'd insist on plain English in marketing material. My red pen became legendary as I wielded it and crossed out passive language.

My obsession with keeping marketing simple started after taking part in a strategic review and product development. Remember, I was working for a financial services company.

Product developments in financial services companies often take a long time. There is no, *"Hey, here's a great idea. Let's rustle up a test product and get it out there in a few weeks to see whether it flies or whether it crashes."*

Back in the 1990s, with ancient, creaking mainframe computer systems, things took ages. Eighteen months to two years to build a new financial services product. Something like an investment bond, a unit trust or a life insurance policy devoured IT time and sucked in most of the company resources for months and years.

The amount of money companies had to invest to launch products in those days ran into millions of pounds because of the time it took. And, therefore, they would always want to make sure they were going to make a massive return on that investment. And I don't mean just a couple of per cent. They will often go into set returns on investment of between 10% and 20%.

My company wanted to launch a new form of investment product and it hired a big management consultancy firm to come in and help us with the project. Setting aside several weeks, the directors found a venue out in the countryside that looked like one of those stately homes or manor houses you see in TV murder mystery series, with a long sweeping driveway and expansive grounds and gardens.

Imagine a time before mobile phones – escape from the daily routine was possible. The consultant even discouraged us from using the pay phone to call the office during the breaks.

Each day we arrived, to the aroma of steaming jugs of hot strong coffee and a tray of croissants and Danish pastries. The consultancy firm brought with them a crate full of flip charts, mountains of Post-it notes and piles of coloured pens.

We set about looking at the strategy for this product development and went through the process I'd learned. We did research, we asked questions and we listened to the customer feedback, using it to develop product ideas.

The management consultancy guy was Benjamin. He looked impressive in his pinstripe London City suit, complete with waistcoat and red braces. I half expected him to quote Gordon Gekko and say, "Lunch is for wimps."

Every time he opened his mouth all that came out was a flood of technobabble, management-speak, jargon, gobbledegook and bloated bollocks. I found him ludicrous. But what amazed me was everybody else in the room seemed to lap this up. And over the next few days we spent with Benjamin, everybody else started copying his speech patterns, using the same terminology, the same kinds of words and the same big sentences. Long, rambling, passive voice sentences.

Benjamin took us through the aforementioned SWOT and PEST analyses. We looked at Ansoff's Matrix and Boston Grids. We even touched on Maslow's Hierarchy of Needs, and we analysed all of this to death.

Things got complicated.

We took part in a Post-it note exercise – a painful process which would become a staple of my experience with big corporate strategy over the next couple of decades.

Everyone scribbled frantically, heads down. The scratching of pens on Post-it notes became the only sound in the room, apart from the ticking of the grandfather clock.

Benjamin invited us to stick the Post-it notes on flipchart paper he'd hung on the walls around the room.

Once we had hundreds of notes stuck on the paper, we stood back to admire our work and Benjamin thanked us for our ideas and arduous effort. He then asked us to rearrange the notes under different sub-categories. We performed this rearrangement many times.

Later, we brainstormed in pairs and then moved into breakout rooms to brainstorm in groups. We drew conclusions from the SWOT and PEST analyses, looked at the customer feedback and came up with product scenarios. We considered development plans and timescales. What would we need to do to launch this to market? What resources would we need?

Leaving the country house behind us, we returned to the office and normality settled upon us – until two weeks later, when Benjamin came back.

He'd written up a lengthy document of about 100 pages, regurgitating most of what we'd written on those Post-it notes.

He stood up, red braces exposed, and announced, "I think we've got the basics of some exceptionally excellent product ideas here." And he said, and I'll never forget this sentence, "Now we must finesse the paradigm to achieve maximum alacrity." Yes, seriously. Here it is again.

*Now we must finesse the paradigm to achieve maximum alacrity.*

I could see some of the other members of the team sitting there, tongues hanging out, as they lapped up this nonsense, while I was thinking, "What a load of bollocks."

We must *finesse the paradigm*. What's wrong with *refine the idea?* It's what he meant. Does *finesse* and *paradigm* sound more *professional?* Does it sound more deserving of the high price tag placed on Benjamin's services?

I wasn't even sure what *alacrity* meant. I assumed it was a posh way of saying *clarity*. Had Google been available then, it would have told me Benjamin had misused the word completely. Benjamin was my introduction to the gobbledegook world of management consultancy.

I'm sure I planted the seed for my *cat sat on the mat* presentation segment way back in Benjamin's sessions. It just took 20 years to grow and blossom.

Here's another example from a marketing conference a few years later that gave me more fuel for my developing anti-complexity obsession. Another speaker, let's call him Tony, came up on the stage. His subject was insurance products. He started his speech by saying something provocative like, "The product is dead! We must change the *paradigm.*"

*Paradigm.*

I don't know whether somebody had bet Tony about how often he could use the word *paradigm*, but he used it as many times as he possibly could in his speech. He would pause every few slides and say, "We need to change the *paradigm.*" Or, "We need a different *paradigm.*" Or, "The *paradigm* is exhausted." One time he laid it out, word by word. "We. Need. To. Change. The. *Paradigm.*"

I waited, maybe prayed, for somebody to put their hand up and say, "What the fuck is a *paradigm?*" In the end, it just made him look foolish. Why do we feel, especially in professional industries, we have to use such claptrap?

The word *paradigm* haunts me to this day.

Later, when I found myself leading teams, I'd start calling people out in meetings if they used clichéd management-speak phrases. For example, an IT person might say, "I don't have the bandwidth for this."

I'd grin and ask, "What's wrong with 'I'm busy'?"

I think some of these people probably thought I was just an irritating wanker. But here's the thing. If you ask other businesspeople what they think of management-speak mumbo jumbo and jargon, most will criticise it, call it out and have a laugh about it. They laugh about it, but they still use it.

I once asked for examples of cringeworthy management-speak in a post on LinkedIn. Hundreds of people replied and posted their own examples. Here's one.

My personal favourite is **methodology**, which, of course, is the study of methods. What methodology did you use? I bloody didn't! I used a *method*, for Christ's sake.

And some more.

Where to even start? Let's circle back on that. Can you reach out to him? Let's take a helicopter view of this. Let's run it up the flagpole. We should pick the low-hanging fruit. That tech is bleeding edge. Let's square the circle.

The non-word **decumulation** gets right on my norks.

Anyone who uses the phrase **customer journey** can quite frankly get in the sea.

And don't even get me started on people that say, **going forward**.

I must admit *customer journey* is one of my own favourites. And no one should *reach out* unless they're a member of the *Four Tops*.

It's not just management-speak mumbo jumbo and jargon. Bloated language finds its way into corporate copy, and internal and external communications can become blighted by big words and pointless phrases.

For example:

*We recognise there is a learning gap here that requires a knowledge transfer piece.*

And:

*We conduct effective root cause analysis and have a cross-functional feedback loop to drive structural solutions to continuously improve customer satisfaction while reducing operational cost.*

I once received an email from a marketing agency wanting to set up a meeting. The depth of bloated language shocked me. Here's one of the many incredible sentences:

*Our unique, proven and collaborative approach of combining doctorate-level theoretical analytics, strategy and world-class creative execution delivers ground-breaking, game-changing initiatives for ambitious brands.*

What on earth did it mean? Was it supposed to impress me? Do they really think I want to do business with people who produce such codswallop?

Here's another one from my gibberish file:

*Key to this is shifting the business from a product sales-led focus to an approach based on end-to-end customer experience and data-driven insight, as well as moving beyond the rational economics behind much traditional financial communication, towards creating a positive emotional resonance in customers with innovative engaging marketing using innovative digital channels and capabilities.*

That's as clear as day, isn't it?

Whatever industry you work in, whether it's an industry of complex products and processes like financial services, or a simple one selling cupcakes, we owe it to our customers and each other to make products, processes and communications simple.

After nearly two decades of fighting complexity at both the strategic stage of marketing and the communications front end, I've rebooted my career as a consultant and speaker, from which my signature *cat sat on the mat* story developed, helping people keep their marketing simple.

My mantra is:

- have a strategy before you get to the tactics;
- keep it simple.

Shall we make marketing simple? Let's get into it.

# A simpler way to do marketing strategy: the Offer–Goal–Activity model

The full marketing discipline taught in business schools and in textbooks can be daunting and appear complex. It's still valid, and some of the best marketers in history have used this process with enormous success, building successful companies and launching profitable campaigns.

But for those without marketing qualifications or long marketing careers, this process can appear complex and blighted by some of the issues we looked at in earlier chapters. Here is a list of the components of the academic marketing model so you can see later how my simple model achieves the same thing. I'm not trying to replace the traditional model, but I do believe mine is simpler for people without marketing backgrounds.

- Customer focus
- Research
- Strength Weaknesses Opportunity and Threat (SWOT) analysis
- Political Economic Social and Technology (PEST) analysis
- Customer segmentation
- Targeting
- Positioning
- Strategic purpose and goals
- Revenue and budget
- Product or service
- Price
- Distribution
- Communications (including advertising, promotions, social

media)
- People
- Brand

That's the traditional academic way of looking at it.

Now let's look at something I call the Offer–Goal–Activity model. It's something I put together over my years in big corporate and used in the background to keep me sane and prevent me from drowning in a swamp of complexity. For a long time, it lived in my head, stored away ready to pop out when I needed a quick way of getting back on track.

Senior management might dump a large strategy document on my desk and ask for comments, or a colleague might ask for my thoughts on a piece of literature or a page for our website.

I found I could whip out the Offer–Goal–Activity model and apply it to the task in hand, big or small. A bit like a pre-take-off checklist for a pilot, it became my machete to hack through complexity.

The model allowed me to simplify everything, but I never wrote it down. Not for a long time.

Not until I left big corporate, became a consultant and started helping people with their marketing strategy. Not until I started speaking at conferences again.

Using it with my consultancy clients, I found it worked equally well with companies needing help to develop a full marketing plan for a suite of products as with those looking for support with a specific piece of marketing material. The model started making regular appearances in my conference speeches and on my podcast.

In summary the model works like this.

## Offer

This is your product or service. What it costs and why it's better and different to all your competitors. You'll put it together from a total understanding of the needs of your customers.

As you put together your offer you'll focus in on your key messages and one-liners to describe your offer. Dare I say, your *elevator pitch*. No, let's not use *elevator pitch*. It's a cliché and is almost management-speak mumbo jumbo.

You'll also look at the content you'll need to put together to answer the questions customers will have about your offer.

## Goal

The goal is your business aims: to increase sales, to make a certain level of profit, to engage with a certain number of customers. Within the goal you'll also think about budget. How much do you have to spend on your marketing?

## Activity

Once you have your offer and your goal, you can start to put together your activity. This could include advertising, other content, social media, email and salespeople.

And that's the Offer–Goal–Activity model.

It really is that simple. Put the model side by side with a more traditional or academic marketing framework and we'll find it fits as follows: The Offer and Goal parts are the strategy, and the Activity is the tactics.

Instead of saying, "Let's put together a marketing strategy," you can now say "Let's put together our marketing offer, goal and activity."

It's the same thing without the traditional language or the academic stigma. It removes the corporate bureaucratic complexity. And it works, as I've said, for a full marketing plan or for just one piece of marketing material.

Offer–Goal–Activity becomes an easy discipline for all your marketing jobs, big or small. With it, you can avoid the modern trap of thinking marketing is just about communications. That would be just the activity and it's not enough. Always have a marketing offer, goal *and* activity.

Discussing the model with one of my business mentors prompted him to ask me whether I should create an acronym for Offer–Goal–Activity.

It was a fair question. Many other business authors, not just in marketing, have invented cool acronyms to summarise their ideas. A sales model called SPRINT, for example, where each letter stands for a stage in the process, or a marketing process called SUCCESS.

Looking at the Offer–Goal–Activity model, nothing occurred to me. *The OGA Model* is meaningless and not memorable. Although, given I'm also a yoga teacher in my spare time, maybe I could have come up with a section beginning with Y and called it the *YOGA model*!

My mentor suggested putting the Goal section first, giving us the *GOA* model, and thinking up a fourth section starting with an L, so I could use *GOAL*. That sounded good – result! Except using the acronym *GOAL* where the G also stands for Goal just felt a bit dumb. And I couldn't for the life of me think of a section beginning with the letter L. In the end, my business mentor burst out laughing. We couldn't believe we were doing this.

First, acronyms, especially three-letter acronyms, epitomise the complex world we live in. They are a symptom of bloat, bureaucracy, management-speak mumbo jumbo and just plain muppetry.

To create a new TLA – sorry, three-letter acronym – to describe my model, and to force the last letter to mean something, felt hypocritical given my obsession with keeping things simple.

I've been a bit flippant in these last few paragraphs, but it's deliberate. By writing it down I think I've shown how silly it can be when you try to force an acronym to fit a model. I can just imagine a big company spending weeks of management time agonising over whether it's GOA(L) or (Y)OGA. It's a symptom of the complexity surrounding us.

So, I've saved the world from yet another three-letter acronym. And you can now get on and put together your marketing offer, goal and activity.

# A quick word about brand

Brand is also an important part of the marketing mix. I could write an entire book just on the subject of branding because, like marketing itself, brand is a deeper subject than many people realise.

Earlier, I suggested if we were to go out on the street and ask people for their definitions of marketing many people would give the answer *advertising, promotions and communications.*

Ask the same people on the street what a brand is, and many people will say it's a logo, colour scheme or font. They'll be able to tell you about the *McDonalds* big yellow M, or the *Starbucks* Green Mermaid, *EasyJet's* bright orange aircraft, or *Nike's* swoosh marque.

But just as marketing is more than just advertising, promotions and communications, so brand is more than logos, colour schemes and fonts. Sure, the logos, colour schemes and fonts are part of it, but a true brand takes time to develop. It's also about the products and services you offer and how they resonate with customers, and the experience customers have when they deal with you, both positive and negative. A brand is also what people say about you or your business behind your back.

If you're starting in business, or looking to get serious with your marketing for the first time, and don't have an established brand as such, then going through the Offer–Goal–Activity model on the coming pages will also give you the building blocks of a brand. In a later chapter, I'll cover how you can use the work you've done on your offer, goals and activity to feed into your brand, should you want to.

If you're an established business, you might already have a brand based on your existing vision, mission, offer and goals. You can use these existing insights to work on your Offer–Goal–Activity marketing plan. And it never hurts to review your position anyway.

If you're just starting out, your vision and mission might develop out of your Offer–Goal–Activity work, or you might already have some ideas. Whatever the reality, for the purposes of this interlude into branding, let's look at what vision and mission mean.

A vision is where you want to get to at some point in the future. It's where you'll be when you've completed your mission. It may not just be where you want the company to be but where you want your customers, or indeed the world, to end up.

A vision could be: By 2025, every family in Manchester will enjoy Lynda's Cupcakes as a weekly treat.

A pharmaceutical company might have a mission to *Cure testicular cancer by 2030.*

One of the most famous vision statements was Microsoft's: *A computer on every desk and in every home.*

If a vision is where we want to be in the future, a mission describes how you'll get there. It's the *who*, *what* and *why* of how you'll fulfil your vision. And as we'll discuss in the chapters to come, the *who*, *what* and *why* is our offer. That's why the Offer–Goal–Activity model is so powerful. You can apply it to your overall marketing strategy, or a single piece of marketing communications or, in this case, a vision and mission statement.

Lynda's mission to fulfil her vision of every family in Manchester enjoying her cupcakes will involve:

Who? – the people of Manchester

What? – introducing more people to our delicious cupcakes. They zing with flavour but are made from healthy ingredients and can still be part of a sensible diet.

Why? – although a bit more expensive than other cupcakes, we use 100% natural ingredients for flavour. They're a treat, but we've kept them healthy, so you won't feel guilty.

Lynda can come up with a joint vision and mission statement for her cupcakes company that might read something like this:

Every day we'll introduce more of the people of Manchester to Lynda's Cupcakes. We'll let them experience our delicious cupcakes that zing with flavour, which we make from healthy ingredients. Although our cakes are a little more expensive, we'll explain to our customers how we use 100% natural ingredients for our incredible flavours. Lynda's Cupcakes are a treat, but we've kept them healthy, so our customers won't feel guilty. By 2025, every family in Manchester will enjoy Lynda's Cupcakes as a weekly treat.

Having sat in many corporate meeting rooms for weeks on end agonising over the words of corporate vision and mission statements, and seen the huge amounts spent on brand consultants, only for the statement to end up hidden in plain sight on a wall ignored by everyone, including the senior team who agreed it, my advice is not to spend too much time crafting these words.

In fact, all you have to do is complete this sentence. "I'm on a mission to…" or "We're on a mission to…"

Make it a work in progress. Be 80% happy with the words and involve your team as you put it together. Review it often, but ensure it drives your activity. Keep it simple. Let's bear in mind your vision and mission as you start to put together your Offer–Goal–Activity marketing plan.

# Part two: Offer

# The components of an offer

The offer is your product or service. It's what you sell. It's what you'll become known for. Depending on what it is, people might aspire to own it or make use of it. It's what brings in the money and makes profit.

Depending on the stage of your business you might already have an offer, and that's fine. You could miss out this part of the book or, more usefully, you could use it to refine your offer and strengthen the messages you'll go on to use in the activity.

You rarely hear about product development these days in the context of marketing. It's another casualty of the modern obsession with marketing just being about communications. Unless you have a compelling product or service, and you know why it's better and different to any other company's equivalent, then you haven't got anything to talk about – you haven't got anything to 'market'.

Getting to a product or service that stands out from any other company's equivalent comes from the deep understanding of your customer: their likes and dislikes; their aspirations and fears; their hopes and desires. It comes from an appreciation of their needs and their problems and creative solutions to those needs and problems.

To work on your offer, you need to build the understanding of the customer alongside a comprehensive knowledge of what everyone else does. We need to understand the customer, the market and the competition. And to do this we need research.

This is where things can get complex. Remember Benjamin and his Post-it notes and paradigms that needed finessing?

For the Offer–Goal–Activity marketing plan you must still understand the customer, their needs and problems, the market and the competition. Although without the giant budgets of big corporate you'll have to find some cheaper and cleverer ways to do research and get the quantitative and qualitative results we need.

We can achieve broadly the same as the SWOTs and PESTs and grids and matrices by answering four simple questions:

- Who is your customer?
- What is their problem?
- How do you fix their problem better and different to anyone else?
- What's the minimum you must charge for it?

Can this really give us as good a result as all those academic exercises? Yes.

Answering questions one and two means you must define your customer. The traditional approach to this is to segment the population into distinct groups using certain criteria and then to target the right group for your business.

We still need to do this to get to the offer but answering those questions doesn't mean we have to get bogged down with marketing jargon like segmentation and targeting.

To me, segmentation and targeting sound too clinical, as though it's a scientific study to find a segment of nameless people to flog stuff to. Find out who to target and then bombard them with communications until they buy from us or tell us to get lost.

With the Offer–Goal–Activity marketing model you want to delight real people with your products and services.

# Customers are real people

Marketing always starts with the customers and they are real people.

But sometimes it's easy to forget they're real people with houses, families, cars, interests, hopes and aspirations. Maybe they become customer numbers on a spreadsheet or in a database. Customer data doesn't have feelings, but real people do. Here's how I first realised marketers must never forget customers are real people.

Whenever I deal with a customer problem, I apply what I call the *Couch Test* to the scenario. I invented the *Couch Test* 15 years ago when I appeared on a TV programme to defend the company I worked for after a colossal mistake we'd made.

The experience started on a Friday morning as I was desperately trying to clear my workload, so I could enjoy the weekend ahead. The phone rang, and I found myself talking to a lady from Independent Television (ITV) in the UK. She was a researcher from a TV programme called *We Can Work It Out.*

A consumer affairs programme, it was a champion for customers let down by companies, messed about by corporates, scammed by cowboy tradespeople or ripped off by fraudsters.

The usual format of the show was a live studio segment at the time of broadcast, with video story inserts involving the customer. They'd invite someone from the offending company to get a savage grilling on live TV.

The lady on the phone told me about a customer of ours – we'll call her June – who had claimed money on her critical illness insurance policy. Doctors had diagnosed June with multiple sclerosis, which her policy covered. She put a claim in, but our claims department had turned it down. The reason they gave was June hadn't told us in her application that, many years earlier, she'd had a bout of prolonged pins and needles. If she'd told us this, it's unlikely we'd have given her a policy because prolonged pins and needles can be an early sign of multiple sclerosis.

65

Insurance companies call this misrepresentation. And so, we decided not to pay June her £100,000.

The producers of the TV programme had already shot a video about June and they wanted someone to appear on the show to put forward our reasons for turning down June's claim.

Dropping the phone, I sprinted along to the claims department to find out what we'd done and why. June's file was a huge pile of paper, with dozens of letters, typed notes, Post-it notes, forms, charts and doctors' reports. I discovered almost a year had passed between June claiming and the claims people saying, "No."

Next was a meeting with our PR expert, Tracy. The most pressing question to answer was: do we go on the show or not? Do we send them a statement to read out, or do we just ignore them?

Tracy said, "Someone needs to get their arse on the show."

She took us through her thinking. "It's a live TV show," she said. "If we just send them a statement, they'll read it out, but in such a way that it'll make us look bad. They'll most likely edit the statement too and make us look worse. They can choose to use only a few words from the statement and craft it to support the narrative of the show. We could decline to appear at all or decline to comment, in which case we're effectively admitting our guilt and they'll tear us apart. We'll have no opportunity to defend ourselves. Or we can go live on the TV and try to put our case across."

She let it sink in for a moment.

"Now, as it's a live TV show, they can't actually edit as it's going out. There won't be a delay. What we and they say gets broadcast as is. So, if we can get a word in and explain our position, we might have a chance to put our messages across. But bear in mind everyone watching will see us as the big corporate bad guy."

We then had to decide who was going to appear on the TV show. It's usual for companies to send a senior important person – the CEO, managing director or marketing director.

But they decided they would send me. Everyone said I was a good communicator with a good chance of putting across the company's viewpoint.

All I could imagine was me as an inexperienced gladiator, wearing only a loin cloth and going up against warriors with pikes riding in chariots with swords attached to the wheels.

Tracy spent the weekend before the TV show training me how to handle the upcoming interview.

First, she told me what to expect at the TV studio. "They'll make you feel like the bad guy. But they'll treat the customer like a VIP."

Hearing this information didn't exactly fill me with confidence. But Tracy assured me she'd build my confidence once we'd gone through our messages.

She introduced the concept of the three key messages. Her advice was to come up with three and stick to them.

Tracy spent the rest of the weekend training me, trying to allay my fears and build my confidence, and we came up with our three key messages.

*We couldn't pay June's claim because she'd misrepresented her health history on her application form. 'Misrepresented' is insurance company speak for 'lied'.*

*We wanted to give an example the audience would understand, like someone who had an earlier conviction for drink driving but hadn't told the insurance company about it when they were applying for car insurance.*

*We don't make such tough decisions without a thorough process and discussion. But we must think of all our customers, especially the ones who do give us the correct information on their application forms. Wouldn't it be unfair to them if we paid June her money?*

Sleep eluded me for most of the weekend. I worried incessantly about appearing on the TV show. In my head was a horrible image of me sitting in a baking hot studio. Sweating on camera meant looking guilty on TV, amplifying the 'bad guy' image the TV producers wanted to sell to the viewers.

The following Monday I travelled down from Edinburgh to Yorkshire to the TV studios. One of our PR assistants kept me company on the train. When we arrived at the studio, the TV producers kept us waiting for ages. Nobody said much to us; they didn't even give us much of a briefing about what to expect.

From the waiting area I could see a giant couch where I would soon sit next to the presenter.

I could feel my heart pounding in my chest. My breath felt short. I started to feel those little prickles of sweat popping up on my forehead like tiny bubbles.

The presenter appeared, strode across the studio and sat down on the couch. As the make-up artist put the finishing touches to her make-up and hair, she looked immaculate.

My slot on the show began. The presenter introduced the story. In a grave voice, she explained how my company had declined a big insurance claim for a nice lady called June, suffering from multiple sclerosis.

Next came the pre-recorded interview with June in her home. She looked frail; a seriously ill lady wronged by a big corporate. While they transmitted the videotape, they marched me up to the couch and sat me next to the presenter.

Once the video finished playing, the presenter turned and launched straight into me. "Well, this is outrageous, isn't it?" she said. "Why are you not paying the claim?" I opened my mouth to reply, but the presenter raised her voice and spoke over me. "This lady's paid her premiums for many, many years. She took this policy out so she would get money if she became ill. And now she's ill. And you've let her down. You're not paying the claim. What's going on?"

Despite her aggressive tone, I no longer felt nervous. My greatest fear, of sweating on camera, disappeared. To my surprise, the studio was ice cold. I'd expected tropical but found arctic. I wasn't going to sweat. I felt confident as I recalled the weekend of endless rehearsals about our key messages.

I turned to the presenter. "Unfortunately, she didn't tell us about the pins and needles she had before she took the policy out. Had we known about it we wouldn't have accepted her for a policy in the first place."

Of course, the presenter flew into a fury and started to challenge me on this. I came back using the argument about car insurance.

"This isn't car insurance," the presenter interrupted.

"No, but I'm using the example of car insurance to explain to your viewers how similar rules apply to life and health insurance."

Then the presenter said our client just made an innocent mistake. She hadn't intended to be economical with the truth.

"The pins and needles have nothing to do with the illness. You should pay the claim. Immediately."

My boss had told me under no circumstances could I say we would change our decision and pay.

The TV presenter pushed me further. "Are you going to pay the claim?"

I tried to deflect it again by going back to the misrepresentation. Time seemed to slow down. The spotlight was on me and the questions kept coming. They seemed to be extending the segment until they could get me to say yes or no. They weren't going to cut the segment until I answered.

She must have asked me five times, and all I could think about was millions of people watching this TV show. Watching me, this scumbag insurance person, squirming and avoiding answering a simple question.

She asked me again, "Are you going to pay the claim?"

And I finally said, "No."

Of course, this allowed the presenter to finish the segment with withering condemnation of my company. "So, there you have it, ladies and gentlemen. They're refusing to do the right thing. I don't think it's the last we'll hear about this."

They bundled me out of the studio. No thank you or goodbye. Almost kicked me up the arse to propel me on my way.

When I arrived back at the office the following day everyone hailed me as a hero. The CEO phoned and said he thought I'd done a remarkably good job.

But despite the pats on the back and my perceived personal victory, two million viewers saw the moment on live TV where I'd said no, we were not going to pay. Did it feel like a victory? I began to feel bad.

What happened next was a massive internal enquiry review of June's case that we should have completed before they sent me in front of the cameras. Going through the mountain of paper, we discovered lots more information we hadn't considered before the show. The executive committee of the company decided we were, in fact, in the wrong and we should pay June's claim.

Two weeks later I went back on the TV programme, this time to tell them they had been successful in getting us to change our mind. The second appearance wasn't quite as bad as the first. Well, they'd won, hadn't they? Now they could afford to be nicer to us.

As soon as I sat down on the couch for the second time, they ran the videotape recording of the show two weeks previously. The video of me saying, "No."

And then, live to millions of people, I said, "Yes."

I felt awful. Not because we'd changed our minds and paid. I'd read all the review paperwork. I agreed with the executive committee. But because we'd let the customer down in the first place.

My TV experience forced me to convince the CEO we had to go and visit June and personally hand over the cheque and apologise for the upset we'd put her through. And by *we,* I meant the CEO himself, not just a representative of the company.

Finally, he agreed.

June lived in Scotland, not too far away from Edinburgh, and we drove up to meet her. Her home was a beautiful cottage at the end of a street in a small village at the foot of the Scottish Highlands. Frost sparkled on the ground. We knocked on the cottage door and June let us in.

Sadly, she did look as frail as she had in the video, but she welcomed us into her home, with no animosity at all showing on her face or in her attitude or voice.

We could smell baked bread and in the living room a pile of logs glowed in the heat of a roaring fire. A giant ginger cat sprawled out in front of the flames, enjoying the warmth. What a lovely home.

June offered us coffee and soon the smell of roasted beans combined with the aroma of the bread. We sat down on her sofa, and the CEO apologised and handed over the cheque. June was so nice to us that I felt worse just then than I had done in the TV studio.

That was the moment it occurred to me that over the course of the last year, when we'd been dealing with June, all she had been to us was a problem. She hadn't been a real human being in our eyes, she'd just been a policy number: 1567432G. She hadn't been a real person; she'd been a stack of paper.

Now, here I was, sitting on a comfy sofa in her living room. This was the real person, the real June, baking bread, brewing coffee, with her cat in front of the fire. The person we should have been talking to all along.

We'd let her down. A real person with a real life, and a real life now blighted by illness. We were the bad guys. I was a bad guy.

At that moment, I conceived the idea of the *Couch Test*. I never wanted to go on TV ever again to justify bad service or nasty things perpetrated by a company I was working for.

The *Couch Test* is a question I'd ask myself when faced with a similar issue. Could I go on TV and sit on the couch next to the TV presenter, in front of those spotlights, and legitimately argue we were in the right?

If my answer was, "No, I couldn't," then the issue would fail the *Couch Test*, and I would insist the company do the right thing for the customer.

The *Couch Test* has become my marketing conscience.

# Who is your customer?

I felt it was important to share June's story and how she made me realise, all those years ago, that we must think of our customers as real people. Not names on a list, not policy numbers, not entries in a filing system.

Real people. With real lives, needs, desires and fears. With families, friends and colleagues. Careers. Things they love doing and things they don't.

Our business success comes from the deep understanding of these real people.

Many modern marketing experts suggest putting together an *avatar* of an ideal customer. Some call this a *customer profile* and I've heard others refer to it as a *buyer persona*. Perhaps the correct term is simply *our ideal customer*. I like that one. What do you think?

But one note of caution. Is using terminology like *avatar* and *buyer persona* just another method of categorisation, in the same way as an entry on an email list or a customer number is? By all means let's use these terms to describe our ideal customers as we put together our Offer–Goal–Activity marketing plan. But let's not lose sight of the fact the customer is always a real person. What we call them doesn't matter, but what does matter is defining whose needs our products and services are meeting.

Some of the buyer personas out there are incredibly detailed, with companies creating an imaginary individual and building a whole imaginary life for them. Customer avatars have names; it amuses me how companies come up with bland, slightly old-fashioned names such as Burt or Mabel.

They try to make the avatar as authentic as possible by asking and answering many questions about them. How old are Burt or Mabel? Are they married, single or co-habiting? Do they have children? If so, how many and how old are they? If not, are they planning to start a family in future? Where do they live – which town or city and what neighbourhood? Do they own or rent their house? How much of a burden is their mortgage?

The customer avatar will define Burt and Mabel's occupations and the level they've reached on their career paths. It will define their annual income and whether they are comfortable or stretched financially. It will also have plenty of information about their educational background.

Some will define Burt and Mabel's favourite hobbies. Which TV shows do they watch? What would you find in Burt and Mabel's *Netflix* and *Amazon Prime* watch history? Which books do they like to read? Do Burt and Mabel have any heroes? Which social media platforms do Burt and Mabel hang out on?

And in trying to get deep inside Burt and Mabel's heads as part of putting together the customer avatar, companies will start to look at their goals and aspirations. What are their values, maybe even their political persuasions and social views?

The next part of the process of creating a realistic customer avatar is to try to get inside the head of this imaginary person.

It's an in-depth piece of work, and it's a valid exercise. If you go through this process it allows you to start thinking about the needs Burt and Mabel have.

Obviously, insight into those needs will ultimately let you work out which products and services can meet those needs. These are the products and services that'll give you the business advantage you need to engage with the real-world equivalents of Burt and Mabel and sell them your stuff.

But this is where a warning bell goes off.

Marketers are often guilty of projecting their own thoughts, desires, needs, wants and frames of reference onto their customer personas.

I do it too.

We can't help it. We've been ourselves for our entire lives, and to a certain extent we assume, or wish, other people were the same. And, therefore, we can't help projecting ourselves onto our ideal customer's profile.

Now, undoubtedly there will be people out there just like you, with the same values, needs and desires. But they may not be your ideal customers. It's difficult, but you must divorce yourself from your own personality and create a genuine, ideal customer profile you can work with. You must look out of the window and find real people out there, rather than looking in the mirror and seeing yourself.

Marketing professor and *Marketing Week* magazine columnist Mark Ritson describes this problem as *marketing orientation*. His contention is marketers are the worst people to understand the needs of their customers because their own knowledge of their industry, their beliefs and desires clouds their view of the customers' reality.

If you are to overcome this marketing orientation and understand the genuine needs and wants of people, then you have to get out there and talk to them. Otherwise you risk creating an imaginary figure that is more a personification of yourself than of your potential customers.

Here's an example of this marketing orientation from my days in big corporate. My boss asked me to attend an event in London, where the marketing directors of various companies were meeting to find ways to improve the public's perception of the industry.

Arriving at the rather plush offices of the meeting host, I noticed straight away the attendees were mainly middle-aged and male. Most were in their late 40s and 50s, wearing suits and ties.

The meeting began with the chairman saying we were there to come up with ideas on which the entire industry could work together to improve customer feelings about financial services. How could we increase levels of trust and make the public feel better about a sector blighted by mis-selling scandals and bad publicity?

And that's when it hit me.

Even though I was probably one of the youngest in the room (at the time I was in my late 30s), I realised everybody there had similar backgrounds, career paths, salaries, political leanings, hopes and desires. We weren't seeing the financial services industry as the man on the street sees it; we were seeing it through our own eyes, with our own prejudices and our own *marketing orientation*, as Mark Ritson would say. We were all part of the problem. *I* was part of the problem.

And here we were, proposing those same people could suddenly, magically, solve the problems they had been involved in creating. The same people cannot continue to do the same things yet expect different outcomes, but this is exactly what was happening in that room.

We hadn't invited any customers to the meeting – perhaps we feared the home truths they might tell us – and we hadn't done any research before the meeting to at least have a real customer voice at the table.

So, yes, create an ideal customer profile. Create a buyer persona or avatar. But do some research as well. Talk to real people. Get out on the street with a video camera or an audio recorder and find out what real people think. You need to talk to people outside your social circles, in different cities, in different towns and outside your own comfort zone.

If your ideal customer persona is going to help grow your business, it must be more than just a projection of yourself.

## Zooming in on the customer

Once you've put together your ideal customer profile, the next step is to work out the size of your target market – the number of people who need your product or service. It's good to know how many people there are in your target market, as this will give you an idea of how many of your products or services you can sell.

From this, you can work out how much it will cost to make the product or service and the price you can charge for it, so you can get an idea of the profit you can make from meeting the needs of your ideal customer.

Not everyone in your target market will be identical to your ideal customer. My friend John Espirian, the relentlessly helpful technical copywriter who's built himself a large following by giving tips on how to use LinkedIn, describes his ideal customer as the bullseye on a target.

I like this analogy. Imagine an archery target with a big red bullseye and several other coloured rings surrounding it.

The red bullseye stands for your ideal customer. They show all the personal traits, pain points, values and needs you've laid out in your ideal customer profile. But it's likely that people in the rings surrounding the bullseye will also show enough of the characteristics of your ideal customer profile to make it worth engaging with them, as they may well need your product or service too.

Once you start missing the target completely then you need to adapt your marketing activity because you'll be talking to the wrong people.

How can you get a feel for the size of your target market?

For a local business working out of premises, such as a shop, hair salon or restaurant, then obviously local population statistics will help you work out the size of your target market. You'll be able to get a feel for the demographics of the population, such as their age, and start to match them to your ideal customer profile.

For online businesses and those trading nationally or internationally, it can become trickier to size the target market. One thing you can do is use the functionality in Facebook Ads. The beauty of this is it allows you to include the demographics, interests and desires of your ideal customer.

The first stage of using Facebook Ads' functionality shows you the entire population of Facebook users, which, at the time of writing, amounts to 2.5 billion people. This is obviously a ridiculously high figure to go after, and you need to whittle it down to a market we can cope with.

So now we can start playing around with the factors Facebook considers when finding the people we want to target with our Facebook Ad. You might put in an age range, a country, or a town or city in that country. The number of potential customers drops to a lower amount.

Add in interests and desires and other criteria and suddenly you'll have a potential customer base of manageable size.

Suddenly you've hit the target – and hopefully the bullseye too.

Thanks to Facebook Ads' functionality you now have a promising idea of the number of people fitting your ideal customer profile and how big your target market is.

It's essential to go through the exercise of putting together your ideal customer. I don't obsess over the intricate details of the characteristics of the person in the bullseye area, but I still think it's important to define these to a reasonable level of detail, because this gives us the other rings around our bullseye, which are just as important.

I've worked for companies where customer targeting wasn't exact enough. When you don't create a specific target market you just end up missing the bullseye and the surrounding rings more often than you score a palpable hit.

Saying something like, "Our customer is everyone in the United Kingdom," is plainly ludicrous, and it's equally stupid to claim your target market is millennials – although we do read of many companies who seem to aspire to this ridiculous target. Yes, millennials have certain characteristics, values, thoughts and opinions, but we are talking about an entire generation of people: billions of people. There could be 15 to 20 years between the youngest and oldest millennial.

And those billions of people live in different countries, so their likes and dislikes differ. They have different political motivations and different social attitudes. Some are single, some are married or cohabiting. Some will be rich while others will be on the breadline. There will be millennials who like rock music, millennials who like hip-hop and others who prefer dubstep.

It's impossible to set such a broad target market, even for massive corporates with an unlimited marketing budget. Going after an entire generation means we'd have to make our offer and activity so generic as to make it unremarkable. It's setting yourself up for failure.

You need to understand the needs of your customers and define what makes your product or service better and different from the equivalent from your competitors. You cannot create an in-depth understanding of the needs, aspirations, desires and pain points of an entire generation of billions of people.

Stick to your clearly defined ideal customer. That's the person you're talking to, the person you need to understand. That's the person whose needs and aspirations will guide your product and service development. They'll guide how you set yourself apart from your competitors and they'll ultimately drive your marketing activity.

# What is their problem?

Now you've found your ideal customer, your target market and the size of the target market, it's time to ask, "What is their problem?" We could also ask, "What are their needs?" I've seen this referred to by other marketers as 'customer pain points'. Neither the word *problem* nor the phrase *pain points* is ideal. They both conjure up negative images, and customer needs aren't necessarily negative.

A customer may feel hunger pangs mid-morning at work. The problem they face is they are hungry, and the opportunity for the company is to deliver the solution to their hunger in the form of food – perhaps a different form of healthy snack rather than chocolate bars or potato crisps. The customer need is something to satisfy their hunger pangs. If you describe it as a problem, then the problem is mid-morning hunger pangs. The solution, or the product, is something that sates hunger better than anyone else's solution.

I guess, despite the negative connotation, describing it as a problem or a pain point at least allows you to put together an answer to the problem or pain point, and most people understand problems and solutions.

The best way to find out what problems our customers face, what their pain points are, is to talk to them. And that means research. Good old-fashioned research.

## Why research?

Once again, people often perceive research as another of the complicated dark sides of marketing. Academics, and marketers in big corporates, will talk about qualitative and quantitative research, research questionnaires involving hundreds and thousands of people, and focus groups.

All these approaches are valid. Many of the best marketing campaigns in history have detailed research underpinning them, with answers to thousands of questionnaires providing data that companies can sift through and analyse for insights. Focus groups can also be an invaluable source of customer insight and feedback. I've been involved in focus groups looking at product concepts, straplines for advertising campaigns, storyboards for actual adverts, and words and images for individual items of literature.

I said before how one of my first bosses was an absolute stickler for research. He wouldn't allow us to put together as much as a one-page sales aid unless we had researched the content, including the words and the titles. Admittedly, we didn't always take these into focus groups. But we always made sure we spoke to some potential customers, even if this was just a few people around a table over lunch.

Personally, I've always been a huge fan of the focus group. I admit it can be great fun turning up to listen to the discussions between potential customers. But we must be careful with our questions, and the group needs a good moderator. I've found people often tell us what they think we want to hear. Or they give us the politically correct answer. They might not want to tell us what they really think, especially in front of other people.

Quite often the venues for the focus groups involve two rooms separated by a one-way mirror. These let the people who commission the research sit behind the mirror and watch the participants talking to each other. For the researchers, it's a window. All the participants will see is their own reflections in a mirror. Usually the moderator of the discussion will let the participants know members of the company are lurking behind the mirrors, but they'll keep the name of the company confidential so as not to bias the discussion. If the participants know which company is conducting the research and they have any negative dealings with the company, it may invalidate the entire discussion if they bring personal grievances into the room or try to influence the opinions of others.

Depending on the topic of the research, you might want to reveal the name of the company to get some feedback or to ask how they feel about the named company offering the product or running an advertising campaign. But revealing the name at the start will bias the discussion.

As good as extensive quantitative and qualitative research is, including focus groups, it is expensive and often beyond the budget of small companies and sole traders. But to put together an Offer–Goal–Activity marketing plan we need to understand our customer needs, so research is essential. We can't build a marketing plan based on guesswork.

In the same way the digital world gives everyone access to communication tools like audio and video through mobile technology, so you can do research at a fraction of the cost you'd have paid 10 or 20 years ago.

Ideally, you should conduct research to discover your customer needs, which will inform how you build your products and services. You should then consider research to check how well your products and services meet those customer needs and how you stand out from and beat your competitors. Once you have your product and service and start to put together your marketing communications activity then, ideally, you should research the language, headlines, straplines and some of the copy you use in the activity.

This doesn't have to be multi-million-pound quantitative and qualitative research with focus groups and massive questionnaires, but you should be speaking to some of your customers all the way through this process.

## The difference between qualitative and quantitative research

Qualitative research gets you a good understanding of opinions, reasons and motivations: you're gathering insights into the problem you're investigating. Focus groups and individual interviews are the best examples of qualitative research.

Quantitative research usually happens after the qualitative research, to gather statistics and data to back up and justify the findings of the focus groups and individual interviews. This type of research often involves surveys, mass telephone interviews and online polls.

For companies with small budgets, it's probably best to favour qualitative over quantitative research. Local businesses can host discussion groups with ideal customers. For the price of a coffee or lunch, they might gain the valuable insights they need. I've heard of chefs who want to open restaurants running cookery classes to try out recipes before opening their doors to paying customers, and fitness instructors and personal trainers can run free demonstrations when developing new classes. Genuine feedback from ideal customers is gold dust when it comes to refining your offer and, most importantly, it helps you identify how you can make it stand out from the competition.

Having massive amounts of data isn't always an advantage, and to get to the insights we need to be able to interpret the data. The Market Research Society says it's better to have a thousand pieces of good data analysed by a human being than a million pieces of bad data analysed by a machine. You need these insights if you are to make the breakthrough that will inform you how you can solve your customers' problems better than anyone else.

## Getting research done

Let's have a look at some of the cost-effective ways you can research the needs of your customers. You can use these same methods later to research how your products and services measure up to and stand out from the rest. And you can use the same methods again to check your marketing communications activity.

First, look for free resources on the internet. For example, many countries conduct a census once every ten years, and local authorities might also have information you can look at. The Royal Mail in the UK has a mass of data available, and you can also try Google Analytics and Facebook Insights.

Second, don't forget a good old Google search. There's a huge amount of information out there about your markets and other markets we're interested in. In fact, the main problem is not a lack of information but too much of it.

When you do research, you're looking for insights that you can use to create a great solution to a customer's problem and a competitive advantage for your business. Be careful to take a balanced view of what you read on the internet. It's easy to find plenty of information to support a certain viewpoint but this can lead to confirmation bias.

What is confirmation bias? It's a tendency people have to seek information that confirms their beliefs. People gather or remember information selectively and then interpret it in a biased way. The effect is stronger for emotionally charged issues and deeply entrenched beliefs. They also tend to view ambiguous evidence as supporting their existing view.

For example, if someone has heard insurance companies only pay 38% of insurance claims, despite the fact they can find many arguments to the contrary on the internet, they will select the articles confirming their viewpoint and deliberately or subconsciously ignore those that conflict with their view. You can see why it is so hard to convince some people of the truth. So deeply entrenched is their belief, they will only acknowledge the information confirming their view.

Confirmation bias works both ways though. As marketers and business owners, confirmation bias affects us too. A financial services marketing person will naturally seek out the information supporting their view that companies pay 99% of insurance claims. Here we have a massive disconnect between what the customer thinks (companies only pay 38% of claims) and reality (they pay 99% of claims).

When using Google to research your markets and come up with your offer, it's important to look at both sides of the argument and not just the information you would prefer to be true.

Third, you can *listen to social media*. Yes, listen.

It might seem like an odd thing to say when many marketers use social media to send out broadcasts, which are effectively adverts for their stuff. But remember, social media developed as a conversational tool before it became a marketing platform and real people are out there having conversations about the things they are interested in, whether that's holidays, food, football or popular culture. They'll also talk about their problems and what products they use to solve them – which are the best and why, which are the worst and why, and how much they cost.

Sometimes, instead of using social media to broadcast, it's best to shut up and listen.

If you have a large following on a social media platform you could start by asking questions and compiling answers. You could take it further and use social media to invite people to take part in a one-to-one interview over FaceTime or Skype, or maybe a video discussion group. You might have to give them an incentive to get involved, such as running a competition or a giveaway. If you keep it local you could arrange a meeting in a coffee shop, pub or restaurant.

Even if you don't have a large following you can still use social media to listen to what people are saying about your market and the products in it. Big corporates watch for keywords based on their brand and product names to get a flow of opinions and data. They'll even watch for misspelt versions of their brands or look for "Brand X sucks".

Twitter has a powerful search engine you can use to fine tune and listen to what people are saying. Imagine we're doing some research on what people think about coffee shops. We can try some of the following Twitter search terms – just bung them in the box.

Search for tweets containing the words:

*coffee shop*

Twitter will give us a list of tweets including the words *coffee* and *shop*. This is likely to be too broad a search term as we'll get results from all over the world, and the words needn't appear together in a tweet. We might find a tweet saying, "I started the day with a coffee. Then after work I went to the barber's shop." It's not specific enough.

To get a more specific response, we can search for an exact phrase by sticking it in speech marks:

*"coffee shop"*

Now Twitter will give us a list of tweets including the exact phrase *'coffee shop'*. It's still likely to be too broad and we'll still get results from all over the world, but the comments might be useful to get a general flavour of what people are saying.

To dig deeper into our country or local area we can include the location in our search. Add in *near:location* to zoom in on where you are:

*"coffee shop" near:UK*

You can dig even deeper into Twitter search and become even more specific. I've included a whole host of useful Twitter search strings in Appendix 1.

Perhaps the most powerful Twitter search tool is the ability to find the questions people are asking about a subject by simply adding a question mark after the search term.

*"coffee shop"? near:Edinburgh*

Twitter will give us a list of tweets where people have used our search term in the form of a question, which gives us an opportunity to jump in and answer those questions and engage with potential customers. But, more importantly, it gives us a list of questions we'll want to address with our activity later.

Good marketing communications answer the questions people ask about products and services. Using social media to listen to what people are asking doesn't just give you insights that can help you put together your offer, it can also guide you in what content and promotional material you'll need to put together later.

The fourth method of conducting research is to send out a *survey*. Thanks to systems like Survey Monkey we no longer need to hire specialist research companies to do surveys for us. We can put together our own questionnaires and either send them to our own email list, if we have one, or take advantage of the customer list offered by the survey company. And we can specify the characteristics of our ideal customer, so we can be confident of talking to the right people.

Systems like Survey Monkey offer free versions, but for the best results you're looking at a small cost for running the survey and perhaps an incentive to encourage people to fill in the questionnaire. During my marketing career I've run research projects with large research companies costing tens of thousands of pounds. Today we could do a similar exercise for a fraction of the cost.

If you have an email list, offering a prize to anyone who fills in your survey is an effective way to increase the number of people who click through. I run an annual listener survey for my Marketing and Finance Podcast. Keeping it short and simple – a maximum of ten questions – it's helped me to shape the topics I've covered and the guests I've invited onto the show. I've offered prizes including quality champagne, business books and cinema vouchers.

Start asking questions and begin to understand your customers' problems.

## Getting to the insights

There are a couple of other things to bear in mind as you start asking questions. When conducting research, it's easy to ask questions to get the answer you want rather than ones that genuinely reveal insights. Imagine an airline that offers complimentary food and drink is looking to change its in-flight service. It could ask a question along these lines:

What type of service would you prefer on your two-hour flight to Spain?
- No food and drink at all
- Food and drink you can buy on board
- Food and drink you can buy in advance and be served first on board

Let's say option b, buy food and drink on board, was the most popular answer. The airline might use it as a reason to stop offering complimentary food and drink as part of the ticket. They might even go out with a press release that says *Our research shows people prefer the choice to buy food and drink on board.* But the research didn't offer complimentary food and drink as a choice. Multiple choice questions and yes/no questions can bias the results.

Remember, we're always looking for insights. We want to try and get to the *why*. Yes, we want answers to our questions, but we want to understand the motivation behind the answers. Asking open-ended questions and allowing people to inject emotion into their answers give us better insights and a greater chance of spotting a breakthrough idea.

Returning to the airline example, by trying to get to the *why*, we might learn that customers would prefer a complimentary meal if the ticket price remained within a certain amount.

People rarely give you their most insightful answer the first time. The real insights come from the third or fourth question. Getting to the real *why* is where we'll find the golden nuggets.

## When the research says no

Sometimes the research you undertake might not give you the answers you were expecting, or the answers you want. This might mean you have to take some decisions you don't like as a result. One example from my corporate career came when we tried to produce a viral video. Yes, I know it's almost impossible to deliberately put together a video that goes viral, but we wanted to produce one and give it every chance we could to get maximum views.

At the time I was marketing director in a financial services company, and I had the privilege of working with a public relations manager who has since become one of my closest friends. For a long time in the late 2000s and early 2010s, Neil Cameron and I were the sole champions of social media and content marketing in UK financial services. We were one of the first teams in the UK financial services industry to use Twitter. We set up a blog site and were early experimenters with video, although this was long before video became possible using mobile technology – we still had to employ an external company to produce videos for us. Looking back, I now realise Neil and I were pioneers in our niche. We just didn't know it.

Lacking the budget for TV advertising, we still felt we had enough money to put together a short film that we hoped would become popular on YouTube and social media. At the best of times financial services is a very dry subject – few people get excited about pensions and savings. And we were working in the sector of the market dealing with life insurance policies, perhaps the dullest, least interesting financial services products for most people.

We felt whatever video we shot had to be hard-hitting. Perhaps it needed to be controversial, or at least rib-achingly funny. It had to raise eyebrows. But we also needed to be mindful not to offend anyone.

Life insurance policies obviously pay out after people die. These are difficult and emotional periods of time for families, so striking the right balance of message and tone in the film would be difficult.

We briefed several agencies and asked them to put together scripts we could use in research to test the idea with potential customers and financial advisers. The standout script was indeed funny. The first time I read it, I laughed out loud. Zombies featured prominently in popular culture at the time. *The Walking Dead* was in its early seasons and zombies seem to be cropping up in films and other media all the time.

The scenario presented by the script asked us to imagine an office setting – think of the TV series *The Office*, starring Ricky Gervais and Martin Freeman. In fact, the agency asked us to imagine Martin Freeman speaking the words we read in the script, along with his trademark comic timing.

The script described a typical office environment. We could see desks where people sit working away at PCs. In the corner a zombie is busily hammering away on his keyboard. He doesn't look too healthy. He's got pale white skin, black bags under his bloodshot eyes, and raggedy hair.

The script then introduces a lady from HR who asks to speak to the zombie in her office. He shuffles behind her and follows her to her room – as you would expect any zombie in *The Walking Dead* to do.

The HR lady asks the zombie how he's feeling. The zombie shrugs.

He isn't feeling too good. He's dead, after all. He scratches his nose and part of it falls off. HR Lady looks embarrassed.

The script reveals the zombie can't afford to stop working even though he's dead. His family need the money he brings in from his salary. When he was alive, the zombie never took out life insurance and therefore he must carry on working to make ends meet.

The banter between the HR lady and the zombie is hilarious.

However, you can see at once the potential problem – it's black humour. And it's a massive risk offending people if you start talking about death in such a way.

But the script was funny. Everyone who read it agreed it made them laugh out loud. Everyone who read the script thought the video would have a good chance of becoming popular on YouTube and social media.

But most of them also highlighted we'd find people who the video offended and there could be a backlash. Was it something our brand was willing to take a risk on?

As you would imagine, those of us involved in putting the script together were keen to go on and shoot the video. But we agreed it was important to take the script and the concept out to research, so we ran a few focus groups and played the script out to groups of customers, journalists and financial advisers.

In the end, the script proved to be like Marmite. The people we researched it with either loved it or hated it. We did dig deep with the questioning, trying to find out the *why* behind their answers, which included much emotion. We were tackling a tricky subject, after all.

The results revealed about 80% thought the video was funny and would raise awareness amongst consumers of the need for life insurance. They thought the film would appeal to middle-aged men, particularly those who watch the *Dave* TV channel.

But 20% of the people we talked to thought it was offensive and that we were making light of death. They wondered what people who had been recently bereaved would think of a company portraying a much-loved father as a zombie.

A high-profile journalist in the UK financial services industry commented he thought the film was hard-hitting and would certainly make people think about the subject. He concluded his comments by saying he thought we'd be brave indeed to shoot it and put it out there. He also wished we would go ahead but didn't envy us the backlash.

Given the 80/20 split in feedback, what would you have done?

When you know there is a potential downside to a product, a marketing campaign or a piece of communication, you can always plan to take care of the people you know it's going to upset.

Any good marketing or PR person will always have plans in place to react to the negatives as well as the positives. In fact, it would mark you out as being strong in your communications if you had a plan to take care of those people you knew would be upset or offended by a communication campaign.

But we were in the early days of social media becoming more mainstream, and we'd seen examples of brands stumbling into crises by making ill-considered comments on social media.

Neil and I put together a plan for how we would roll the film out and how we'd use it to spread the word about how important life insurance could be. We also drafted detailed plans on how we would handle the negative reactions.

The higher-ups within the group of which we were part focused, as you would expect, on how we would deal with the negative attention the film might generate, but in the end the risk was just too much for the company to take. With regret, we agreed to abandon the zombie script and look for another idea.

Looking back, we took the right decision not to go ahead with the zombie film, given the nature of the business we were in. As I said, death is a difficult subject to approach at the best of times. And as edgy as we wanted the film to be to have the best chance of going viral, it crossed the line – we didn't want it to go viral for the wrong reasons.

There have been quite a few controversial films over the last few years, including those from *Pepsi* and *Heineken*, and it makes me wonder whether they ever took their ideas out to research like we did and if they listened to the research findings before deciding to put their film out into the public domain.

Do the research. Listen. And then act upon the results.

# How do you solve their problem better and different than anyone else?

Now you have your research, you're well on the way to that deep understanding of your customers and their needs. Now you can start to find answers in the form of products and services that can meet their needs and solve their problems.

A word of caution. Sometimes you must remember, however articulate your customers, that often they don't know what they want or, more accurately, they don't know what they can have.

B Karl Benz invented the motorcar and Henry Ford found a way to make them available to the masses. If you'd asked customers what they wanted from transport their answer would've been "Faster horses."

The key to high-quality product and service development is gaining insight from customer research and then making a jump to create something profoundly different, or even unique. Benz made the leap from animal (the horse) to mechanical (the car), and we want to achieve the same insight to develop our products and services.

On the surface the results of your research and the comments made by your customers may not point to anything remarkable. If you're the owner of a hairdressing salon, asking your customers what their problems are reveals predictable answers. Their hair gets dull with split ends, or they're not happy with the colour or style of their hair.

The answers to their problems are treatments to moisturise their hair, give it shine and banish split ends; to change their colour, which will enhance their image and self-confidence; and to give them a new hairstyle for a wedding or social event.

If you're the owner of a garage, it's likely the answers to your customer questions will be similarly predictable: cars break down, people need the engine fixing or they need a MOT check or an oil change. Maybe someone pranged them, and they need the dent in the bodywork beating out and respraying.

Whatever line of business you're in, whether you're offering a physical product or a service, it's likely your research gives you predictable responses. Most people face the same problems, and there are hundreds of people out there offering similar answers to those problems in the form of products and services.

This leads to two issues.

First, it becomes difficult to genuinely come up with an offer that stands out from everyone else. And second, it creates a culture of mediocrity across many industries.

Let's look at an airline industry example again. Before charter flights took off in the 1970s and before the low-cost airline boom of the late 1990s and early 2000s, air travel was a luxury offered by national flag carriers.

Charter airlines started to take people on package holidays to the Mediterranean in cramped planes, but scheduled airlines like British Airways had a near monopoly on scheduled domestic and long-haul routes. The national carriers' fares were high, especially on those long-haul routes, and people saw airline travel as a luxury available only to those with deep pockets.

But then the low-cost airline model changed everything. Airlines like easyJet and Ryanair in Europe and Southwest Airlines in the US started offering cheap fares, making airline travel available to everyone. Now, 20 years later, many low-cost airline companies compete against each other and most of the national carriers, at least on their short-haul networks, have also adopted a low-cost airline model.

While low prices have driven this industry development, the reality is there is nothing much to differentiate between the carriers other than the colour of their logos. Most airlines cram as many people into as little space as possible, and the seats are rock hard, uncomfortable and tight. Passengers must pay extra for baggage and most carriers run a 'buy on board' for food and drink. Many national airlines have stopped giving complimentary food and drink on short-haul flights and moved to a BOB model as well.

Have a look at most short-haul airlines and it seems they are competing against each other to be the same. Even on long-haul flights, where airlines offer business class and first class, the overall products and services are similar across airlines. British Airways revolutionised business class in the early 2000s by bringing in their flatbed seat and now most airlines offer a flatbed seat.

It's the same with trains – just look at the many train franchise companies in the UK. Again, the services they offer are similar. It's easy to gravitate towards a similar offering, but it's also dangerous as often price becomes the only thing people use to choose between them.

It's easy to come up with something that's the same as everyone else. You might be able to tweak it slightly to create a tiny difference, but those differences will be superficial. If you want to work out how to resolve the customers' problems better and different to anyone else, you need to think beyond cosmetic differences, beyond mediocrity. You need to be thinking about how you can stand out from your competitors. It's the next step in putting together your offer.

Now you must dive back into research to better understand what your competitors are doing. And you can use all the techniques we discussed earlier, such as listening on social media, sending out surveys, having one-to-one discussion and focus groups, if you can afford them.

As marketers, your ideas for products and services and how to stand out come from the deep, almost obsessive understanding of your customers. Should they also come from a deep understanding of your competitors?

One school of thought suggests we shouldn't have too in-depth a look at what our competitors are up to. Indeed, obsessing about our competitors can deflect us from our aim of giving our customers a standout product or service. If our analysis and understanding of how other people are solving customers' problems leads us to launching a 'me too' offering, then perhaps it's good advice not to obsess about our competitors.

Might you end up simply trying to create something that beats everyone else in a cosmetic way? Maybe this is the problem outlined in the airline example earlier. Too much preoccupation with everyone else stops you thinking about meeting the needs of your customers and simply makes you think of ways to beat your competitors.

They are not the same thing.

The answers to how you solve your customers problems better and different than anyone else comes from delighting the customer, not becoming preoccupied with beating a competitor.

Imagine a scenario where Company A develops a product to meet a customer need. They launch it and promote its five standout features. Their launch delights customers and they grow their sales and profits. Competitors cast envious glances at this success and move in to steal a piece of the action.

Company B comes up with a similar product but adds in a couple of extra new features. Their marketing activity shouts loud about the differences in features between their offer and Company A's original.

Company C is next to bring out their version and they swell the features list by adding even more.

Concerned about the challenge to its early success, Company A relaunches its product, adopting all the extra features added by Companies B and C, but also adding some more of its own.

Before long the marketing activity from all the companies starts to focus on the features rather than the benefits. They stop thinking of the customer and instead become obsessed with fighting each other over features.

The customer becomes immune to the messages; they don't care.

It creates a *features race* which becomes a marathon without a finishing line. And the reality is no one will win.

If this is where you end up by analysing your competitors, then perhaps it's good advice not to bother.

My view is we must have a good understanding of what our competitors offer to inform our marketing plans, but we need to be careful not to fall into the fight-over-features trap.

Here are some of the questions you need answers to:

- How does everyone else resolve your customers' problems?
- What is like your offer and what is different?
- What does everyone else charge?

Can we work out which differences are just cosmetic and don't really add to the customer experience? Are these features just included to tick a box in the fight over features? Or are they a genuine part of resolving of the customers' problems?

What are your customers saying about your competitors' products and services? What are your competitors saying about their competition, including you? Again, don't allow this research to draw you into a fight over features.

## Competitive advantage

Your analysis of your competitors is important when putting together your offer. Some people would describe this process as 'benchmarking'. Experts and academics have penned books and papers on benchmarking, and it takes up a great deal of time on those awaydays during corporate strategy sessions where everyone has fun sticking Post-it notes on walls.

Use this exercise to inform the development of your product or service, not to steer it. Many boardrooms become more obsessed with beating the competition than they do with delighting the customer. But being better is not enough. Why? Because your competitors can run a similar benchmarking exercise and it won't take them long to overtake you on features and benefits if they're playing the same *better* game.

Better isn't good enough. Better can end up being mediocre. Being different is the way to stand out.

This is true whether your product is a cupcake, a bunch of flowers, a clothing range, a dipping sauce or a garden hose. Or whether your service is consultancy, an online course or a fitness makeover.

So how can you be different?

From an academic point of view there are three main ways to stand out from your competitors, three levers you can pull:

- your product
- your price
- your service

Academic wisdom backed up by commercial reality suggests you can only pull two of these levers at the same time. You might choose to have a high-quality product and sell it at a low price, but the profit margins on this approach would be so low you wouldn't be able to offer a great service.

Or you might choose to have a fantastic product with amazing service. But to achieve it you'd have to charge a higher price than everyone else.

You could go for low-priced and amazing service, but this is difficult. Southwest Airlines in the US, the airline upon which most European low-cost airlines base their model, is well-known for its low prices and amazing service. However, if you look closely it's often the case that prices aren't as low as the marketing likes to suggest. Pulling all three levers at the same time is difficult, and from a profit point of view this third option is the hardest to achieve.

However, in the modern world and with technological advancements, it should be possible for everyone to provide a decent product at a decent price with decent service. The problem is this yet again creates a baseline for mediocrity. It creates an environment where company executives aspire to beat their competitors on tiny differences in features. Again, it creates the desire to be better when being different is the way to stand out.

You can have a better price (a lower price, obviously), but is it different? And playing a price game is never a sensible strategy when low profit margins can lead to bankruptcy. And who knows when your competitors are about to become bankrupt? Why follow them over the cliff like a lemming?

You can aspire for better products but it's an endless race run for years with the finishing line constantly moving ahead of the leaders of the pack.

You can aspire for better service, but what is good service? I still think it's possible to stand out here and be different. People don't like waiting in queues or on phones; they don't like rude staff, clunky processes and inconvenience. But again, it's easy to fall into the 'better' trap as opposed to being different and standing out.

What can you do?

As well as looking at your competitors, another source of insight can come from looking outside your own environment. What are people doing to solve problems in other industries, which you could transfer to your own?

I once read about an airport looking to improve its queue management. Check-in lines spilled out of the doors into the car park. Security queues took an eternity and created anxiety among people fearful of missing their flights. They looked at how efficient Disney were with controlling lines in their theme parks and adopted Disney's methods in the airport.

Once you've collected a load of data you must start to look again for the insights. At a conference once, I got talking to a dentist who was looking for a way to stand out from his competitors. We chatted about his customers and I was delighted to find he had done a great deal of thinking about their needs and problems. But he admitted he was stumped for a while as to what his offer could be.

He'd asked the question *Who are my customers?* As you would expect for a local business, his customers came from his local area and were a mix of private patients and those covered by the UK's National Health Service.

The *What are their problems?* question revealed all the answers you would expect. People got toothache and tooth decay, and they had stained and crooked teeth.

But, in trying to find a way of meeting his customers' needs better than anyone else, he found his products and services were identical to other dental practices.

He could find the cause of people's toothache and try to fix it. He treated tooth decay with fillings and crowns. He could polish stained teeth, add white veneers or, again, use crowns. And he could straighten crooked teeth with braces. But every other dentist in the area could do all these things as well.

In the practice was a waiting room with receptionists. They sent out text reminders for patient appointments. They handed children 'good patient' badges. He'd looked at his prices and didn't want to get into a price war.

Then an insight hit him.

His initial thinking focused on the problems people had with their oral health and hygiene. During a conversation with a patient he heard something that changed his whole approach. It was another problem most people have. They just don't like going to the dentist. Many people hate going and even fear the visit.

They dread reclining in the chair with eye-guard glasses on their heads and bibs around their necks. Swilling their mouths out with the weird-tasting pink mouthwash. The nippy prick of the anaesthetic needle and the high-pitched whine of the drill. The vibration through every bone in their body as a fast-rotating drill hits tooth enamel. Some people will even put up with toothache and stained teeth rather than overcome their fears and go and sit in the dentist's chair.

Our conversation moved on to how he started trying to solve those *fear* problems his patients had, as well as the ones relating to the health of their teeth.

He changed the whole image of his practice.

Gone was the typical sterile waiting room with piles of tatty, well-thumbed and out-of-date magazines. He created a pleasant sitting room area instead, with chilled lemon water in a dispenser with real glasses, mood lighting, music and the subtle scent of aromatherapy in the background.

Instead of the harsh white clinical jackets most dental receptionists wear, he kitted out his people with shirts and trousers in pastel shades that didn't give off a *dentist* vibe.

When customers walked through the door, their first impression wasn't of entering a typical dentist's reception and waiting room. It was of going into a health spa. He found the different environment put his patients at ease and allayed some of their fears. The health spa vibe continued into the surgery rooms as well.

He gave his patients stress balls to squeeze and placed large collages on the ceiling, giving patients something to do and to look at, to take their minds off the treatment.

By changing the environment and solving a problem people have with dentists – not only by doing it better, but by doing it differently from any of his competitors – he became much sought after, both by those people lucky enough to get on his NHS list and by those willing to pay to become a private patient.

When you understand your customers' problems and find the element of a product or service that genuinely makes you stand out, that golden nugget can be the turning point.

By answering three questions – *Who is your customer? What is their problem?* and *How do we solve their problem better and different to anyone else?* – we've achieved as much as corporates and academics would do with their traditional marketing strategy models.

Let's recap.

We've defined an ideal customer profile allowing us to target a specific group of people.

We've researched their needs and come up with solutions to those needs in the form of products and services.

And we've worked out how we meet those needs better and different than anyone else by researching our competitors.

Before we move on to consider the goal and activity phases and start getting people to buy our product or service, we need to do two more things.

First, we need to decide how much to charge for our product or service. And second, we need a summary of our offer we can use to create messages we can feed into our activity.

# What's the minimum you must charge for it?

Pricing is one of the most important things to think about when putting together your offer. You're in business to make money. Even if you're a non-profit organisation, you must bring in cash to cover your costs.

We're still going to look at pricing as part of the activity phase of the Offer–Goal–Activity marketing approach but, from experience, I want to include the base price within the offer. Our base price will allow us to cover our costs and make a profit that fits in with our goals. We need to know the base price we must charge before we can start thinking about activity like discounts or price promotions.

I'll hold my hands up and admit that even in my most senior roles as marketing director and managing director, pricing was the area of marketing I found hardest.

Maths, or "sums", as I like to call it, has never been my strong point, but it's vitally important you understand the numbers. If you don't understand it yourself, get someone on the team who does understand it. Get friendly with them. Nurture them.

My economics and marketing education at school and university taught me the very basics of pricing a product. Work out the cost per unit of the product you're making, and there is the price you must charge to cover those costs. Anything you charge above the amount is profit for your business.

As an example, if it costs you 60p to make a chocolate bar and you can sell the chocolate bar for £1 then you'll make 40p profit per bar.

Of course, it's rarely that simple. Some products will be a combination of many separate components or elements, each of which will have its own price. Costs will not only include manufacturing expenses but transport, storage and packaging. There'll be promotional marketing costs and possibly taxes or duties.

I learned about pricing in a financial services company selling long-term savings plans. Most of these involve the customer paying a premium each month, sometimes over periods of up to 40 years. Working out the price to charge each month and then the profit on a long-term product is difficult, so financial services companies employ extremely clever people called 'actuaries' who can do the necessary calculations. Actuaries consider interest rates now and expected interest rates in the future and then discount back the value of all future payments to work out the profit for each price point. To a maths ignoramus like me, these calculations seemed like a black art. Actuaries also make many assumptions in their calculations, and sometimes these lead to problems.

When I was high up in one financial services firm, my executive team and I had to report to the group CEO and finance committee every three months. They called this the Quarterly Review, or the QR for short. Another horrible corporate acronym.

The sessions gave the group CEO and the finance people a chance to question the financial direction of each business unit, measuring current profit and expected future profits against goals. As an important part of the business cycle, QRs could be intense grilling sessions. It was like being under the spotlight in an interrogation, and I felt the financial people in the room were deliberately hostile.

In the run up to one QR my actuarial team ran the numbers, and we were delighted to find we were ahead of target for premiums and £2 million ahead of our profit target. Good news like this meant the QR would be a positive one, perhaps allowing us to explore other business opportunities and investments.

Then, a few days before I was due to hop on a plane down to London to sit in the glare of the QR spotlight, the group financial people announced a change to the pricing assumptions. My actuaries reran the figures and we were horrified to find we were now £1.5 million under our profit target, even though we were hitting the numbers for our sales.

The QR became an uncomfortable confrontation with the CEO and his finance people about what steps I was going to take to make up the deficit. In less than 24 hours I'd gone from being £2 million ahead to £1.5 million behind. Just by the stroke of an actuary's pen.

When the CEO asked for an action plan on how we would increase sales to cover the loss, I wanted to say, "Just go back to the old assumptions and we'll all be happy again, you muppet." At that moment, I realised what a black art financial services pricing is, and why the people in charge of financial services companies are usually accountants or actuaries. They're the only ones who can understand these complex sums. Or they're the only ones who can wave the magic wand to change the assumptions and create the numbers they want.

It was an important lesson. Be on top of the numbers, however hard it is, and if it is an area of weakness for you, get help.

Hopefully your product or service won't be as complex as those long-term savings. Maybe you're looking at a course, some consultancy, cakes, flowers or widgets. Something much simpler. But being on top of the numbers is still important. Let's have a look at how to come up with a robust base price.

When you put together your offer, the first question you should have asked was *Who is your customer?* As part of the research to answer the question and come up with an ideal customer profile you'll have formed a good idea of what your ideal customer will pay for your product and service. This knowledge will inform your base price work and help you come up with pricing promotions later as part of your marketing activity.

You'll then have asked, How do we solve our customers' problems better and different to anyone else?

To get to the answer, you'll have done some more research. *What are our competitors doing and how can we not only be better, but different as well?* The research will have given you a good feel for how much competitors charge. If you've genuinely put together something better and different then you should be able to charge more for your product or service. Or at least have scope to at some point.

When looking at what competitors charge, it's important not to become seduced into simply charging the same price or undercutting them. You don't want to start a price war, because price wars eat into profits. They commoditise your products and undermine the work you've done to ensure they're better and different than your competitors'.

Armed with knowledge of what your customers might be willing to pay and what your competitors charge you can come up with a base price for your products and services.

First, let's work out your fixed and variable costs.

Fixed costs are those that don't change depending upon the number of products or services you sell. Premises rent and software licences are examples of fixed costs.

Variable costs change depending upon the number of product units you make or services you supply and will include staff costs, materials and components, promotional costs, postage, utilities, storage and transportation.

Once you know the costs involved in building or putting together your products and services you can come up with a base price. This is where you want to include an element of profit.

My favourite method is **cost plus pricing**.

Imagine you're building Orange Widgets.

| | |
|---|---|
| Fixed costs | £50.00 |
| Variable costs | £100.00 |
| **Total cost** | **£150.00** |
| Profit we want (25%) | £37.50 |
| **Base price** | **£187.50** |

This is a profit margin of 25%.

There are other pricing methods, such as **mark-up pricing**, when you add a fixed extra amount to the costs rather than a percentage of profit. Or **demand-led pricing**, when you allow the price to flex depending on the demand for the product. **Competitive pricing** is where you set your price based on what your competitors charge. Companies tend to price commodity products in this way.

Once you have your base price and are happy with the amount of profit this generates, you can use this when planning your activity later.

There are times when you might want to offer a discount on the base price, perhaps as part of a launch offer. Changing the price is one lever you can pull to affect the volume of sales, along with content, promotions, advertising, PR and sales activity.

Your aim should always be to cover the cost of production, or of supplying a service, plus some profit on top. Just covering costs (breaking even) should be a minimum goal, but there may be times when you can justify reducing the price even lower. We'll look more at pricing when we get to the activity section of the Offer–Goal–Activity marketing model.

# Summary of the offer – and the one-liner and reasons to believe

You have an offer. Now let's come up with some simple words that explain what it is and why it solves your customers' problems better and different to anyone else. Academics, corporates and agencies call this the Customer Value Proposition, or the Customer Benefit Statement.

Let's keep it simple. You know your offer because you've answered those three important questions: Who is our customer? What is their problem? And How do you solve their problem better and different than anyone else?

Let's aim to come up with a one-liner to describe your offer and a few support statements for the one-liner to back it up. These could include the reasons people should believe you.

Later, when you plan your activity, which could be advertising, content, social media, email and other methods of communication, one way you'll come up with those communications will be to answer the questions your customers will have about your offer. Your *one-liner and reasons to believe* gives you a useful crib sheet to refer to when you put together your communications.

Another way you can solve your customers' problems better and different to anyone else is to have better communications than everyone else. There's so much bloated, complex communication out there. Communicating simply is a way to engage your customers and make them like you and trust you enough to buy from you.

Simple can be part of the *different* that makes you stand out.

You're looking for a simple description of your product or service and the main benefit it offers. If your product or service has many features, it's easy to make this one-liner too complicated. Let's aim to keep it as short and simple as possible. One of my favourite product one-liners in the history of marketing is for a cleaning product called

Domestos.

The one-liner goes as follows: Domestos. Kills all known germs. Dead.

I remember this from my childhood, and as I wrote this chapter, I assumed Unilever, the company behind Domestos, must have moved on to another slogan by now. But I checked on Google, and they're still using that one-liner today. It's simple, which is why they've used it for so long. And it works.

By reading the one-liner, we know instantly what Domestos does: *it kills germs*. It might have been tempting, when putting together the one-liner, to try to include more information about the product. Unilever may have wanted to tell their customers Domestos was a household cleaner. Or they may have wanted to use the word 'bleach'. Perhaps they were tempted to include some of the chemical compounds contained in the Domestos formula in the one-liner.

But they decided to stick to one of the most important product benefits: *It kills all known germs. Dead.*

Most people can infer from the one-liner that Domestos is a cleaning product. And they can easily work out that if they use it to clean their house, they can expect to kill all known germs. Dead.

Just consider the simplicity of the statement for a moment. It's the sort of one-liner you should aspire to for your own products and services. No complexity. No padding. No fluff. The Domestos one-liner is obviously a marketing slogan, but it's so good it also fits the bill as a product benefit statement, a one-liner.

There've been many other incredible marketing slogans over the years that have passed into culture and urban legend. Ronseal's *It does exactly what it says on the tin* is another notable example. Unlike the Domestos slogan, however, unless you know Ronseal is wood stain for sheds and fences, you won't be able to work it out from the slogan alone.

For your one-liner you want to put across the main benefit of your product or service so it's obvious to your customers.

Have a go. See if you can do it in one sentence. Don't worry about trying to also make it sound like a snappy marketing slogan or strapline; that can come later.

Once you have your one-liner you can move on to create some reasons why your customers should believe it. It's important to highlight how your product and service solves your customers' problem and does this better and different than anyone else's. But you do need to take care you don't get too focused on the features of the product here.

As we found earlier, one of the mistakes some companies make in the marketing of their products and services is focusing too much on features and not enough on benefits. There's a crucial difference between talking about features and talking about benefits.

Talk about features and you shine the spotlight on the product – often on things the customer doesn't understand or care about. Even if your product or service has an impressive list of features, you must try to extract the customer benefit from those features and express how these benefits solve the customer's problem better and different than anyone else.

When you talk about benefits you shine the spotlight back on the customer. Sales books talk about selling the sizzle rather than the sausage. Selling the hole rather than the drill bit. It's good advice, but I always like to take it further and express the benefit in term of the problem it solves.

Going back to the household cleaner example, one of the features of our bottle of bleach might be it has a fresh lemon fragrance. To describe the fresh lemon fragrance is to describe a feature of the product, not the benefit.

Throughout my career as a marketer I've always looked at features and ask the question, "So what?" It's another one of those things my first boss, Steeple Fingers, drummed into me. He was a stickler, remember. When I ran the marketing team and they came along with a product feature, "So what?" was my first question every time.

Imagine the marketers in the bleach company saying, "This bottle of bleach has a fresh lemon fragrance."

So what?

It's the question most likely in the customer's mind. Or, more likely, "What's in it for me?" To successfully convince the customer why they should be interested in the feature, we need to tell them the benefit. And that means talking about the problem the feature resolves.

We already know what these problems are because we researched them and use them while putting together our offer. This is a good moment to think about the emotions and feelings we can draw on to help sell the benefit.

Going back to the bleach, the problem might be a dirty kitchen after a week of cooking, with stale smells and grease building up on the cooker hob and work surfaces.

Clean the kitchen with our bleach and you wipe away the cooking smells and the grease, leaving the kitchen smelling clean and fresh. The hint of fresh lemon fragrance in our bleach will make you feel you're walking in the fresh air outdoors rather than being in a kitchen.

When thinking about expressing the benefits of your product or service, you can use one of the best and most simple marketing formulas. It's known as the Problem–Agitate–Solution formula.

Let's look at each of those parts of the formula. We could think about all the benefits of the bleach, or simply concentrate on one of the benefits, for example, the fresh lemon fragrance. Let's consider first the bleach as a whole.

What's the **problem**?

After a week of cooking your kitchen is dirty and full of stale odours. Dirt and grease have built up around the cooker hob and over the top of the work surfaces. You can smell the grime in the kitchen from everywhere else in the house.

Next, we want to **agitate** the problem in the customer's mind. Perhaps play upon their emotions a little.

The longer you leave the kitchen in that state, the worse the smell will become. What about germs breeding in the dirt and grease? But you're also busy and it just sucks getting around to doing the cleaning.

Now we've expressed the problem, and agitated the problem in the customer's mind, we focus on the **solution**.

Our bleach makes it easy to clean your kitchen quickly. Slap some on a cloth and wipe it over the surfaces. It cuts through the dirt and lifts it instantly – you don't even need to scrub. It kills all known germs, dead. The kitchen will smell fresh and clean with a hint of lemon.

In the example we've clumped a few problems together. The fact the kitchen is dirty, the fact it smells stale and greasy, the fact cleaning the kitchen takes a lot of time, and the fact germs breed in a dirty kitchen. In our solution, we address each of those problems by highlighting the benefits of the bleach.

What about focusing on one feature of the bleach? Perhaps its fresh lemon fragrance?

Here's the **problem**:

After a week of cooking your kitchen's full of stale odours. You can smell the kitchen from everywhere else in the house.

Here's how we **agitate** it:

You know the longer you leave the kitchen in that state, the worse the smell will become.

Here's the **solution**:

After cleaning, the kitchen will smell fresh and clean with a hint of lemon. Isn't it better to be able to detect the gorgeous hint of lemon from everywhere in the house rather than the stale smell of cooking fat? The outdoor smell of fresh air rather than the indoor smell of grime.

See how powerful the Problem–Agitate–Solution formula can be?

And you can use it in all types of marketing communications: blogs and websites, or the scripts for adverts, audio or videos. You can even fit the Problem–Agitate–Solution formula into something as short as a tweet. Look at a few adverts and see if you can spot the Problem–Agitate–Solution formula in action. Sometimes clever marketers can even make the feature part of the communication.

Remember the *Here's the science bit* in the *L'Oréal* adverts? The narrative of many of their adverts followed the Problem–Agitate–Solution formula as follows:

**Problem**: Do you have dull lifeless hair?

**Agitate**: When you've got a wedding or event to attend, you're going to worry about how you look on the day.

**Solution**: Use our shampoo and it'll leave your hair shiny and full of body.

And just before the solution, they hit you with the *Here's the science bit,* where they talk about a feature of the product. The one I always remember is *Ceramide R.* Customers don't usually like jargon, and normally they'd ignore features they don't understand, but *L'Oréal* included an animation showing the Ceramide R seeping into the hair, strengthening it and making it shine.

So, always focus on the benefits. But be clever how you talk about the features if you can find a way to make them enhance your communication of the benefits.

Ideally, try to aim for three reasons to believe.

So now you have:

- One-liner
- Benefit/Reason to believe 1
- Benefit/Reason to believe 2
- Benefit/Reason to believe 3

Now your offer is complete.

# The Covid-19 lesson about the offer

As I was working on the finishing touches to this book, the Covid-19 pandemic took hold and the world changed for everyone.

Through a combination of mainstream media and political briefings, it suddenly seemed like everyone was telling us what to do.

Government advice overall was sensible. Stay at home to stop the spread of the virus.

But from some marketing experts came an avalanche of instructions:

"You need to pivot your business."

"You need to move completely online."

"You need to use this downtime to learn a new skill."

The problem with these statements is that they assume everyone and every business is in the same boat. We're not.

Everyone's and every business's circumstances are different.

Yes, some might have to pivot their businesses, but equally others might find they are twice as busy doing what they've always done.

Yes, some might have to move to a completely online model, but others might not.

Yes, you could use the downtime to learn a new skill, but not if you're suddenly working from home and trying to home school three children.

The Covid-19 crisis just highlights the importance of going through the offer process. In the face of the virus sweeping the world, those who reviewed the four steps to defining their offer, albeit quicker than they might have done in the past, will have been able to decide whether they needed to pivot, go online or stay the same.

What Covid-19 didn't change was the process of simple marketing strategy.

# Part three: Goal

# Setting goals

"They've increased our sales target for next year by 20%," said the regional sales manager for Scotland, as he knocked back an ice-cold pint of Tennent's lager, almost in one gulp. "It's going to be a challenge."

I drank half of my pint as a sign of commiseration before adding, "And they've cut our marketing budget by 20% as well."

The sales guy ordered another couple of pints. "For fuck's sake. If we're going to hit our sales targets, we're going to need you marketing guys to do even more to help us."

Targets. Objectives. Goals. My first experience of these in business was the annual planning cycle in big corporate, which usually took up three long and painful months. In my junior roles the company spared me the detail of the awaydays, the Post-it note sticking sessions, SWOTs and PESTs, grids and matrices.

I, along with the rest of my non-management colleagues, usually found out the results of those three gruelling months when the senior managers, visibly exhausted by their ordeal, presented the targets for next year. The sessions followed a predictable format.

Someone, probably the MD or CEO, would stand up and deliver a motivational review of the previous year. If we'd beaten our target there'd be congratulations and the hint of a bonus to come. The high-ups might even hand out a glass of wine or a cream cake. If we hadn't reached our targets the presenters would analyse what had stopped us and what the management team were going to do to overcome them.

The sales director would review highlights of the sales campaigns. Perhaps they'd talk about specific deals or new relationships. The marketing director would remind us of the year's marketing activity, including advertising campaigns, sales support and public relations. The finance director always seemed to speak the longest when reviewing the year, and I remember little about what he said. In the days before smartphones the only escape from a dull finance presentation was to doze off. Finally, they'd hit us with our targets for the next year.

Before I climbed the ranks within the organisation it seemed to me, sitting there listening to the management, all they'd done in their three-month planning process was to take the previous year's targets and budgets, add a random percentage to the target and subtract an equally random percentage from the budget.

"For next year, we're increasing our sales targets by 20%."

"For next year, we want you to cut your budgets by 20%."

When I had climbed the ranks within the organisation and got to take part in the three-month planning cycle, I discovered my impression of the process was spot on the truth. They *did* just take last year's targets and add a random percentage increase. And they *did* just take last year's budget and subtract a random percentage from it. Of course, coming after the awaydays of Post-it note sticking sessions, SWOTs and PESTs and grids and matrices, there was an illusion they'd based these decisions on robust analysis.

After setting the targets and the budgets came the hardest part – putting together the plan to achieve the increase in sales and the cut in budgets.

For us in marketing it meant looking at product developments and campaigns. What could we do more of to help sales meet their targets? What could we cut back on or stop doing? Could we become more efficient? Could we change to a cheaper printer to save on print costs? Or should we just start using a lower grade of paper? No one really cares whether we print our client guides on 'sky silk' or 'bog standard' paper, do they? Do we really need to travel down from Edinburgh to London as often as we do to meet journalists? Could we not just pick up the phone?

From the targets and the budgets would come our personal goals. We'd agree our SMART objectives. Some of these SMARTs would relate to the sales targets and budget cuts. Others would be more personal, for example, develop your project management skills.

When I was a manager, I was the one dishing out the SMARTs. I tried hard to make the process as painless as possible for my people, to get them to set their own goals and then agree or refine them together. I disliked the process, both as a junior and as a senior. So much management time seemed devoted to setting and reviewing SMARTs. Was it 10% of everyone's time over the course of a year? Maybe closer to 25%? I often wondered what the time, tallied up across the organisation, cost. And whether it really helped the company meet its sales targets. "What would happen," I pondered over another pint of Tennent's, probably with the same regional sales manager, "if we did away with the PDD process, ditched SMARTs and used the money on marketing and sales activity instead?"

Despite these experiences of setting targets and the cascade of SMART goals, I'm a fan of goal setting. It's an essential business process and can help focus everyone in the company on what they need to do to make the business a success. I even like the idea of SMART goals. Yes, it's another acronym I associate with management-speak mumbo jumbo. But the principle is sound.

All too often, though, the corporate machine makes the process too painful. They turn it into a box-ticking exercise rather than one that genuinely helps the business to succeed. In the Offer–Goal–Activity model, goal setting is important. But when we're putting together our marketing offer, goal and activity, let's keep it simple. It shouldn't be a painful process and it certainly shouldn't take three months.

It should be more than simply increasing sales targets by a random percentage and reducing budgets by another random percentage. It should be something you believe in and can get everyone behind. Our goals should drive our offer and our activity.

# Are SMARTs not so smart?

"We want to increase our sales by 20%" is a fine goal to have. But we can look at many other goals as part of our Offer–Goal–Activity marketing plan.

- Increase customer awareness of our company brand, or our offer
- Grow our market share
- Launch a new offer
- Sell a certain number of units of each offer
- Target a new set of customers
- Improve customer satisfaction
- Enhance customer relationships
- Increase profit margins
- Aim for a specific return on investment on advertising spend
- Target a certain number of people to sign up to our email list
- Get a certain number of public relations mentions

Once you have a goal in mind, what's the best way to record it and make progress towards achieving it? By far the most popular approach businesses use is the SMART goals system I mentioned earlier.

SMART sets the complexity and bureaucracy alarm bells ringing in my head, but let's look at the system for a moment. After all, there must be something in it if so many companies are using it, right?

The letters in the acronym SMART stand for:

**S**pecific
**M**easurable
**A**chievable
**R**ealistic
**T**ime-bound

Looking at each in turn, you can see the sense in the system.

## Specific

Making a statement like, "We want to grab market share," or "We want to increase sales," is too vague.

"We want to grab a market share of 15%," or "We want to increase sales by 10% to £5 million," is better.

We must ask ourselves what it is we want to achieve, exactly, because being specific creates focus on results.

## Measurable

Again, it makes sense. We don't want to set a goal we can't measure or track. We can measure and track most things these days; we can even measure things like customer opinions, goodwill and word of mouth using digital tools. And it's important not only to measure progress against the end goal but also the progress towards it.

## Achievable and Realistic

These go together for me. Once more it seems like a sensible approach. If our market share is currently 1%, is it achievable and realistic to set a goal to grab 15% straight away?

In business, we want to challenge ourselves. But an unachievable goal will set us up to fail, which could be a disaster for finances and for morale. Nor do we want to set a goal so easy it doesn't stretch the business or encourage the team to push themselves.

## Time-bound

Perfectly sensible, again. What is the period over which we want to achieve our goals? Going back to the market share example, if our market share is currently 1% it might be achievable and realistic to grow it to 15% after five years. But in our fast-moving digital world, where things change every day, can we really know enough about what lies ahead to accurately predict what's going to happen five years on? It might be more achievable and realistic to go for consistent increases over a shorter period.

"We want to increase our market share by 3% each year." It feels more achievable and realistic, but is it challenging enough? Well, it's still 15% after five years, isn't it?

So, on the face of it, SMART is a good system to use, but I have several problems with SMARTs. First, the fact I mentioned before – it's an acronym. It's the epitome of corporate bureaucracy and box-ticking. Like Post-it note sticking exercises, SWOTs and PESTs and grids and matrices, it becomes a process people fear. The annual setting of SMART goals becomes a time employees dread. Managers go through the process because they must, and it keeps HR happy. But it's a chore.

Second, in my experience within big companies, SMARTs force people to focus on their own outcomes without considering the bigger picture. A company might have a marketing goal to run a quarterly campaign and increase sales by £2 million, and an individual within the marketing team might have a goal to manage and plan four campaigns in the coming year.

All good so far.

But an individual in the legal team might have a goal to make sure all communications are accurate and don't break any laws. The marketing person becomes driven to deliver their own results – getting those campaigns signed off and out there – but the legal person wants to scrutinise every word of every communication. These conflicting goals could cause tension between them. SMARTs can create conflict rather than aligning everyone in the same direction.

Third, I think SMARTs can create a culture of mediocrity. *Specific* is good, *measurable* works and *time-bound* is fine. But *achievable* and *realistic* are too vague. They're woolly – to me, they're dampeners. *Achievable* and *realistic* can shatter lofty ambitions, pour freezing water on bold actions and sow seeds of doubt. *Achievable* and *realistic* imply not trying too hard, and that striving for mediocrity is good.

Of course, we don't want to set ourselves impossible goals, because we'll fail and potentially lose money, and morale will plummet. But do we want to stifle the desire to be an exceptional performer? Do we want to settle for safe? If we don't challenge ourselves or aim for something that seems unachievable, how will we ever change the world? Or at least the market we work in?

To me, *achievable* and *realistic* push individuals and companies to a safe answer. I can understand why this happens in big corporates. Conflicting management views, politics and different agendas round the management table mean *achievable* and *realistic* become escape hatches. Someone might say, "Do we really think we can hit a £2 million target? Maybe we should scale it back to £1.5 million?" Or another says, "My only concern is…" followed by an argument creating doubt. Those who question whether a goal is *achievable* or *realistic* might introduce enough doubt for you to shrink your goals.

My fourth problem with SMARTs is the most important one: there's no emotional buy-in. SMARTs don't get me excited. They don't fuel my fire, and they don't make me want to leap out of bed in the morning and bound to work, ready to get stuck in. Let's look at an example.

I love public speaking. I love being on a stage, telling stories, sharing experiences and helping people. I don't get up on a stage because I have an ego that needs stroking; I do it because I get excited helping people through storytelling. My fire burns when I see the light bulb go off above someone's head. And the brighter the light bulb shines, the hotter my fire burns. But when I was in big corporate, one of my SMARTs was to present at 20 events in the next 12 months. Was it specific? *Yes.* Though including the size of the events and their locations could have made it more specific. Was it measurable? *Yes.* Achievable. *Definitely.* Reasonable? *Yup.* Time-bound. *Tick.*

But it's *boring.* The SMART objective isn't exciting. I think we need to ditch *achievable* and *reasonable* and inject a heavy adrenaline shot of excitement into our goal setting.

# A more exciting alternative to SMARTs

I don't want to come up with another acronym to replace SMART. This book's all about moving away from such complexity. Throughout the Offer–Goal–Activity model I'm trying to ask questions instead of using acronyms and jargon. So, let's start with the goal itself.

## What is your goal?

Try writing down your goal or typing it up on a computer screen or in an app on your phone. Then let's ask these questions.

## Why is this goal specific?

We're keeping the *specific* element of SMART but making it so crystal clear it's also *measurable* and *time-bound* by default. Going back to my example from big corporate days, here's the goal around speaking at events, with a little added detail.

Speak at 20 conferences around the UK over the next 12 months with audiences of 150 potential customers in each session.

Now I can ask, "Why is this goal specific?" Well, I must speak. It must be me up there on stage delivering the presentation. I'm going to do this at 20 conferences over the next 12 months. There needs to be 150 people in the audience at each venue. And the people in the audience need to be potential customers of my business.

Can I measure whether it's me speaking? Of course.

Can I measure the number of conferences I speak at? Definitely.

Can I measure whether there are at least 150 potential customers in the audience? Yes. I can measure this after the fact but also use this as a way of deciding which conferences to attend.

# Why is this goal exciting?

Continuing with the speaking example, I can say, "I have an opportunity to help 3,000 people with their marketing by putting together a motivating presentation, including stories and take-aways and calls to action. I'll rehearse the speech so it's slick and I'll ask loads of questions to encourage the audience to interact and feel involved. And I'll get to travel to some interesting cities and meet some inspiring people."

Imagine you're about to launch a content marketing campaign. It's a first for your company. Your goal is to publish one blog post a week that answers specific customer questions about your product and leads to 20 enquiries.

Is it specific enough to be measurable and time-bound? Yes. Now think about why this goal is exciting.

We're a new company but we believe we have a product that meets our customers' needs better and different than our competitors. As we plan and deliver this campaign, everyone in the team is going to learn more about content marketing. Everyone's going to listen to the questions our customers are asking and we're going to work together to create engaging content that answers those questions and lets our customers get to know us, so they'll want to do business with us. It's going to be hard. There's a lot of work to do, but we're all learning together. There may be a few bumps along the way, but we'll get better together as we grow together.

Doesn't it sound more exciting than a simple statement about what the output of the goal is going to be? Isn't it likely to get buy-in from the team?

The most important thing is to know, instinctively, whether your goals are believable. Can you believe in them? Can and do they excite you? Indeed, do they inspire you? If you believe and they do inspire and excite you, then this will motivate you and your teams toward being successful.

If you want to include some sort of reality check to achieve a balance between a goal so big it risks failure and one so small it doesn't offer a challenge, ask yourselves these questions:

- Can we definitely do this?
- Have we achieved something like this before with the same resources, effort and investment?
- Have our competitors or other companies done similar things?

Understand your achievements so far. If your sales increased by 8–10% for the last half year, then setting a goal of a 14–16% increase in sales is challenging but fits your reality check. Setting a target of a 25% increase in sales could be setting you up for failure. Some might say it's a ridiculous goal.

Now we have our goal and we know it's specific, and because it's specific we know we can measure it and we know the timescales. We've made the goal exciting because it inspires us, and we believe in it. Now we feel motivated to achieve it.

SMART objectives don't talk about planning. They define the goal, not how to achieve it. This is the next question we must ask in our alternative to SMART objectives.

## What is the plan to achieve the goal?

The best way to do this is to break the goal down into chunks and be consistent with delivery. I admit I'm not a good planner or project manager so I've always made sure I've had someone who can help me with it.

When planning, I like to work back from the goal. If we want to achieve a target at a certain date in the future, often what happens is we end up rushing to complete the goal at the last minute. By working back along the timeline, we can break the goals down into chunks and plan a consistent timeline. Milestones or checkpoints are useful here too. Ask what needs to happen to meet the goal. If it's a financial goal, how many products do you need to sell? If it's to build a client base, how many sign ups to your email list do you need? What are the actions you need to take and who's going to do it? Once you have all this information, put it in a schedule – a spreadsheet, a Gantt chart, Trello, whatever works best – and then check and update the schedule or plan regularly.

## Who will hold me accountable?

The most important part of goal setting, again missing from the SMART model, is accountability. No doubt at a corporate level companies check progress on their targets at least monthly, maybe weekly, depending upon the nature of their business.

This can be good discipline and it creates accountability. However, there's a danger it can become another box-ticking exercise, especially in big organisations with loads of team members. For smaller businesses or one-person businesses, you can receive the accountability you need in various ways.

There are lots of things I don't miss about big corporate. The bureaucracy and complexity. The political manoeuvring, especially at the top. The excess time spent on activities that didn't contribute to growth or improving the bottom line.

What I did like, however, was being able to get up from my desk, wander down the corridor and seek an opinion from a colleague on an issue I was facing, or bounce an idea off another team member, to get help or feedback.

Getting out of big corporate and setting up my own business meant I lost immediate access to colleagues. How can you fill the gap?

First, find yourself a mentor, and second, join a mastermind group. A mentor doesn't have to be someone you don't know. In fact, it can be more of an advantage to work with someone who does know you, your thought processes, your likes and dislikes, what motivates you, and your strengths and weaknesses.

It might seem like a clever idea to target a well know businessperson. We've all dreamed of working with people like Richard

Branson, Warren Buffet, Peter Jones or whoever your business idol is, but it's not going to happen. You're likely to find a good mentor within your existing network. It could be an old boss or colleague, or someone from another company you've worked with before. Someone who knows you, likes you and trusts you.

Joining a mastermind group is possibly a better alternative if you want to work with people you'd class as your peers. I first came across the concept of mastermind groups when I started following serial entrepreneur Chris Ducker's podcast back in 2013. Chris runs large mastermind events, but the concept works well for individuals looking for ongoing accountability.

I went to one of Chris's mastermind events a few years ago. About 50 of us descended on a chain hotel in London, split up into groups of five and listened to Chris explain the rules.

We'd each be in the hot seat for 45 minutes. This was our chance to focus on our business and ask for feedback and ideas from the four other people around the table. Some people were there to talk about embryonic plans for their new business. Others wanted help with their latest marketing campaign. One person on my table just wanted to run through her content calendar. Another wanted to test a segment from her latest keynote speech. Everyone chipped in with ideas, suggestions, advice and encouragement. I came away with a clearer idea of my own offer and where my business was going.

At a more intimate private mastermind with Chris and seven others a year later, we thrashed out the idea for this book.

Mastermind events like Chris's work well when you have a significant business issue or idea you need help with. But if you want accountability, you can set up a regular mastermind group with peers you know and trust. Four people seems the best number, though I've heard of groups with fewer or more.

It's essential to meet regularly – at least monthly, but ideally every two weeks. Each member of the group commits to attending the meetings, usually held over a video conference call on Skype or Zoom, no matter what else is happening in their business lives, bar holidays.

As in the larger mastermind events, each member of the group gets time in the hot seat, which usually means 15 minutes each. Again, the member can ask for help and ideas on a business issue, or just ask to the group to hold them accountable for their goals. Think of the people in your mastermind group as your accountability partners. You can talk to them about your goals, and if you've answered the questions I've suggested for goal setting in this chapter, your group members will have a clear idea of what you're trying to achieve.

   — What is the goal?
   — Why is the goal specific?
   — Why is the goal exciting?
   — What is the plan to achieve the goal?

You can be specific about actions you need to take to meet your goals and talk to them about the consequences and rewards for failure or success.

As you'll be meeting once a month or once a fortnight, you'll have the accountability challenge and the peer help and advice to keep you on target. The answer to the final question, "Who will hold me accountable?" could be, "My mastermind group."

# Budget as part of the goal

In the Offer–Goal–Activity marketing model, we'll consider our budget to be part of our goal.

It makes sense to me. You've set your goal, which is likely to be sales measured in hard cash, or getting to a specific market share, or taking on a certain number of customers.

To meet your goal, you have your offer and will plan the activity part of the model to put together your overall plan. But it's going to cost money to achieve the goal. In the same way you've set a goal of what you want to deliver in terms of business growth, you need to set a goal for money you want to spend to get there.

I'd like you to think of the budget as an investment. Let's think of it in this way:

To meet our goal of sales of £2 million we need to invest £100,000 in our offer and our activity.

My experience of working in big corporate is that the top team – the executives or the C-Suite – never thought of marketing as an investment. They saw marketing as a cost. And every year, as we waded through the three-month-long painful strategy, planning and budget process, the emphasis was on cutting the marketing cost. "How much can you shave off your marketing budget this year?"

I never heard the marketing budget question posed as, "How much do you need to invest in marketing next year to hit our sales target?"

It was always, "Here's our sales target [usually increased] and we want you to cut your marketing costs by 20%." It always left me feeling we had to make do – to reduce the quality of our activity, or to compromise.

Undoubtedly, the accountants felt they were introducing a cost-conscious discipline into the process. But I believe it's better to look at your business goal and work back, and then decide what your offer and activity needs to look like to achieve it. What campaigns will this involve? Is there advertising? Content? Does the product need tweaking? And then get realistic quotes for the work that needs doing and agree it as part of the overall process.

When someone high up tells you how much you can spend, the resulting activity feels like a compromise rather than a properly thought-out plan designed to smash the goal.

In the Offer–Goal–Activity marketing model, try to start with the offer and activity and what it will cost to achieve the goal, rather than starting with an arbitrary amount and working back.

For example, say you set a goal of landing 50 new clients. And say you know for every hundred leads you'll end up welcoming five new customers on board. To get 50 new clients we need 1,000 leads. What activity do you need to plan to get those 1,000 leads?

Arbitrary amounts are costs. Properly thought-out offers and activity are investments. For this reason, we might need to leave setting the budget until after we've spent time going through our offer and activity.

For a completely new start-up, or a business in its infancy, it might be difficult to accurately work backwards from the goal to come up with the best investment in offer and activity. For this reason, it's reasonable to start with an investment as a percentage of sales.

Companies typically start at 7–10% of sales as an amount to invest in marketing activity. It does feel a little arbitrary and, therefore, risks being labelled as a *cost*, but it's a learning curve and the *it's an investment* mindset will win through once sales start flooding in.

However, here are some thoughts on how to get to the investment we need. As always, I like to use questions to find the answers we need, rather than come up with some acronym or formula.

## What does it cost to run your business?

Think about your fixed costs and staff costs. Will you need to take on more people to achieve the goal you've set, or can you get there with your existing team? Will you have to involve an agency in your offer and activity?

129

How much is your offer and activity going to cost?

How much does it cost to supply the physical product or service?

Are you going to use paid advertising? This could include traditional advertising in newspapers, magazines, on TV and on radio. Traditional communications might also include direct mail. Then consider online advertising, such as videos, banner ads, email marketing, pay-per-click (PPC) ads and social media ads (Facebook).

What about marketing material? Will you need to produce any brochures, information booklets, technical guides, customers guides, or giveaway items like T-shirts, stress balls or pens?

How about content marketing, which we agreed was part of your offer, including blog articles, videos, audio podcasts, e-books and webinars?

How much does it cost to put all this together? Think about design, photography, graphic design and agency costs.

And finally, technology and platform costs. Think about the cost of building a website and supporting it, hosting videos and audio files, and email.

So, when setting your budget as part of your goal, ideally work back from your goal to get to the amount you need to invest in your offer and activity. As an alternative, work on investing a percentage of your sales revenue. And please, try to avoid simply setting your budget as "all we have left after we've paid all the other bills".

# Part four: Activity

# Buying process

At last we get to the activity. We can now think about communicating with our customers. We can plan and create advertising campaigns and think about email and social media communications. We can create content, put together pricing promotions and get our sales teams (if we have them) out on the road.

It's worth pausing for just a moment longer to reflect on how important it's been to go through the Offer and Goal stage first. I still believe many marketers dive straight into the activity stage – the communications – without going through the Offer and Goal phases. But by putting the time and effort into clearly defining our offer and goals we can maximise the success of our activity.

You can set yourself up with the greatest opportunity for achieving the goals you set and ensure your activity engages your customers rather than enrages them. By making sure your activity gets customers to know, like and trust you enough to do business with you, you're making certain your activity leads to sales.

Activity leads your customers from being unaware of your offer to having an interest and a desire, then ultimately taking the action to buy.

Once again there are many marketing clichés used to describe this process. Some marketers call this the *customer journey*, but I'm not particularly keen on this phrase. To me, a journey is travelling from Edinburgh to London, or from London to Los Angeles. It just doesn't seem right to describe a buying decision as a journey, nor to describe customer service as a journey. *Customer service* is fine.

Other marketers call this process a *funnel*: a marketing funnel, or a sales funnel. I've also heard people refer to it as a *customer decision funnel*. Again, I'm not keen on the use of the word *funnel* because it doesn't sound customer friendly to me. In my mind, funnels are simply useful pieces of equipment to allow us to transfer liquid from one container to another without spilling the liquid all over the floor. Using *funnel* alludes to manipulation of the customer.

Now obviously we want customers to decide to buy our stuff. But I would prefer our activity to be so engaging they don't feel as if someone has manipulated them. Indeed, our activity must be engaging enough to make customers *want* to buy from us.

So, for the purposes of the Offer–Goal–Activity marketing plan, I prefer not to use the term *funnel,* but we will use a variation of the classic tried-and-trusted advertising framework.

The Attract–Interest–Desire–Action framework is still one of the most powerful for putting together any piece of marketing communications. Whether it's an advert, a blog, a vlog, a podcast, an e-book or even a simple tweet, the AIDA formula works well.

And while this formula works well for communications, you can use a variation of the formula to describe the process customers go through as they decide whether or not to buy.

All you need to do is to change the word *attract* to *awareness.*

Now the process is:

- Awareness
- Interest
- Desire
- Action

And you can extend this process to think about how you keep your customers over the long term and even get them to start talking about your product or services. You want them to become advocates for what you do, don't you? So, add two further parts to the process as follows:

- Retention
- Advocacy

Let's look at each of the stages in a little more detail.

# Awareness

Before the internet and digital tools, the awareness stage depended on advertising or word of mouth. Someone with a problem to solve would look first in their local area – the high street, shops or supermarkets – or they'd ask their friends. They may have referred to a directory such as the *Yellow Pages*. Remember those?

Advertising, particularly on TV and billboards or in newspapers and magazines, aimed to raise awareness of brands and how those brands could solve the customer's problem.

Put simply, a customer in the 1980s might have decided they were hungry and wanted some sweets. But they fancied something other than Opal Fruits, because in all honesty they were a bit maxed out on Opal Fruits. (Opal Fruits are now known as Starburst, of course.) If they had seen an advert for a new Lion Bar on TV or in a magazine, it would have made them aware of a sugary snack they may not have heard of.

Without advertising, they might never have discovered the Lion Bar unless they had physically come across it on the shelves in their grocery store as they were searching for Opal Fruits. Having seen an advert for a Lion Bar, the awareness the advert created in the customer might just have triggered them to buy one when they then saw the snack in the shop. The advert might have also created interest and desire, which we'll come to later.

Once bought and eaten, they might have enjoyed the Lion Bar enough to buy more in future and maybe even tell their friends how much they enjoyed it. Or perhaps they didn't like this new chocolate bar and never bought one again.

Now, of course, it's all different. When someone has a need, or a problem to solve, the first thing they do is turn to an internet search, most likely Google. They might pause to ask their friends by text or messaging app but, for most, Google will be their first port of call. They'll research companies, products and services that can help with their need or problem. When they start searching it's likely they'll type a question into Google: *What's the best UK chocolate bar?* or *What's the newest chocolate bar in the UK?*

Over 70%[6] of buying decisions now revolve around the customer researching companies, brands and products online before making a buying decision. Consumers have unlimited resources on their mobile, tablet or PC screen for this research, and they can check facts, run price and product comparisons and read testimonials without leaving the house. Much of the information consumers use to make their buying decisions is now outside the direct control of the companies that may run adverts for the product or service in question.

Google calls this the Zero Moment of Truth (ZMOT). In the past, when advertising might have raised awareness of a brand enough to prompt the customer to pick up a Lion Bar in the shop, now they are more likely to research up to 20 or more brands, companies or products before making their buying decision. And instead of adverts — especially intrusive or annoying adverts — influencing them, consumers are more likely to be swayed by engaging content in the form or blogs, videos, infographics and audio.

## Interest

Once you've created awareness, either through adverts or content, you need to engage with your customer so they are willing to spend some time understanding your offer in more detail.

Stay focused on the customer's needs by answering their questions, especially those questions most relevant to them individually. Again, this is where content might work best — content that teaches, entertains and inspires people to know, like and trust you enough to do business with you.

---

6 https://www.thinkwithgoogle.com/marketing-resources/micro-moments/zero-moment-truth/ (accessed Jan 2020)

## Desire

As you build interest through your activity, you can also create desire by focusing on what your product and service can do to help the customer. This is the stage to remember the early discussion we had about features versus benefits: the "so what" question.

Let's not talk about ultra-modern shock absorbers on cars. Tell the customer about the smooth ride, even on the bumpiest roads.

Don't go on and on about the fact you offer free home delivery; highlight the fact it saves the customer time and lets them get on with other things. In this example, don't turn the benefit into a chore by making the customer wait at home for half a day to accept delivery.

Instead of saying your broadband offers download speeds of however many GB, say it lets your customer get a two-hour film onto their device in only 90 seconds.

## Action

Once you've piqued your customer's interest and fuelled their desire, you must tell them what you want them to do next. And you must make it easy for them to take that action.

Whether you want them to sign up for an email list, make an appointment to chat on Skype, or just buy your product or service, you must tell them what you want them to do and then make it easy for them to do it.

## Retention

Once your customer has bought your product or service, you want to keep them as a customer. You want them to stay with you and buy more from you in future. An excellent product and an enjoyable experience in the buying process will help with repeat sales, but often you need to consider other methods to get the customer to stay.

Coffee shops use loyalty cards. I have a wallet full of Caffè Nero cards on which you collect nine red stamps you can then exchange for a free coffee. Airlines use frequent flyer schemes that let regular travellers build up air miles, which they can redeem for free flights later. Supermarkets have similar points schemes. My wife saves up her Tesco points all year and cashes them in at Christmas. She often manages to knock several hundred pounds off our Christmas shopping bill in this way.

Customers have so much choice these days, though, that loyalty schemes and special offers only work up to a point. If a company lets a customer down, gives poor customer service or doesn't offer ongoing value for money, then the customer will go elsewhere. Be careful your retention activity doesn't become another process that enrages rather than engages a customer.

Here's an example. One of the online hotel booking sites always sends an email seconds after you've made a booking saying, "London is booked. Where do you want to go next?"

I find it annoying and it makes me think, "Leave it out, I've only just planned this trip. I'll get back to you when I'm ready. Or use someone else who doesn't send annoying emails."

For many years I remained loyal to my car insurance provider and had built up ten years of no claim discounts. These discounts are the main way car insurers try and keep customers. In fact, some customers will avoid making claims for minor damage to their cars rather than lose some of their no claims discounts.

As my renewal date approached, my insurance company sent me a letter telling me what the next year's price would be. They'd put the price up, so I did what any sensible car owner does – I looked on various comparison websites to get a feel for how much the insurance cost elsewhere.

I found I could get a lower price from other reputable companies and I also found my own insurance company offering a much lower price for new customers. I phoned my insurance company and asked them about the difference between my renewal quote and the offer price for a new customer on the comparison website. The agent on the line went straight into 'retention mode' and said they could offer me a discount of 15% on the renewal price. I pointed out that even with the 15% discount, the price for a new customer was still much lower.

Sadly, they were unable to offer me a bigger discount on my existing policy, but recommended I cancelled it and applied for a new one. The difference between the two quotes was big enough for me to go to the inconvenience of filling out a whole new application online for the same company.

They did keep me as a customer for another year. However, I felt angry with them because they weren't prepared to simply give me the 'new customer' price, even though I'd been a customer for ten years.

Another year went by and the same thing happened. This time I was annoyed enough with my insurance company's process to move to a different company altogether. Is this good customer retention? Maybe the insurance company had modelled customer behaviour and could make more profit from the inertia of people renewing without checking alternatives.

But while we all want to make profit, should it drive a process that clearly enrages some customers?

Retention activity can include communications, adverts, price promotions, loyalty schemes and content. Customers will have questions about all these things and it's another opportunity for us to engage with them and delight them.

## Advocacy

Advocacy is word of mouth – and there's nothing new about it. We've been doing word of mouth since before any modern communications devices evolved.

If you like something a great deal, or if an experience makes you say, "Wow!" you're going to tell your friends and family. You're likely to rave about the brand that gave you the wonderful experience or amazing product. You might tweet pictures about it or write reviews on TripAdvisor or another relevant review website. You might even blog about it.

As a frequent traveller, I've written my fair share of hotel and airline reviews over the years. When something impresses me, I feel the need to write about it. For example, a few years ago, I came across a hotel chain called Hotel Indigo. When I'm travelling on business, I have a simple rule. The hotel I'm staying in must at least be up to the standard of my own home.

I've had this debate with travel bookers in the big corporates I've worked in when they've wanted to book me a room in a grubby dive in a remote location. I don't live in a house resembling a prison cell, but nor do I live in five-star luxury with chandeliers and caviar dispensers in my front room. The mattress in my home bedroom isn't made of stone, I don't buy rough toilet tissue and my towels aren't made of bleached iron wool. So I don't want these features when I'm travelling.

But it's not a hard bed and lack of fluffy towels that upsets me most. My three main gripes with hotels around the world – but mainly in the UK – are as follows:

- extra charges for WiFi
- cold, congealed breakfast buffets
- outrageous charges for minibars

I admit charges for WiFi are less common now, but grim breakfast buffets and break-the-bank minibars are still prevalent.

At Hotel Indigo the rooms are quite small, but they are brimming with lovely colourful fabrics, pictures and decorations. But most impressive of all is every room has free WiFi, and a selection of drinks from the minibar are complimentary. At breakfast you order from a menu, they prepare your plate fresh and a waiter brings it to your table. This alone would set Hotel Indigo above many hotels in London. And they are appearing in other UK cities.

I wrote a review on TripAdvisor and on my website about my experience at Indigo; I became an advocate. And I know they appreciated it because they wrote to me and thanked me for the positive review.

In November 2018, I was delighted to be a speaker at the second Youpreneur Summit in London. This event was organised by Chris Ducker, the Mastermind guy I mentioned earlier. There were 350 people in the audience.

My messages, or *value bombs* as Chris Ducker calls them, went down well. You've read some of them in this book already. Chris had seen my *cat sat on the mat* speech before and asked for a new talk for Youpreneur Summit. The result was the entertaining *John the Wineman* story, which I might share in a future edition of this book.

The closing keynote speaker at the conference was Jay Baer, a famous American marketer and customer experience expert. He'd just published a book called *Talk Triggers*. It's all about word-of-mouth marketing, but the title resonated with me. After the conference, I bought Jay's book and started reading it as I headed out to Macedonia for another conference speaking engagement. When I read his chapter on Five Guys, a huge penny dropped in my mind.

Five Guys is a *posh* burger restaurant. It's a bit of a step up in quality from McDonald's or Burger King. They opened a restaurant near us in Edinburgh and my son was keen to experience their burgers, so we went to check it out. I liked the way you could build your own burger, choosing from the toppings – onion, lettuce and gherkin – and the sauces – tomato, mayonnaise and hot chilli.

The server asked if we wanted fries. Now, at the other burger places I mentioned even a large portion of fries seems inadequate. There's often more cardboard in the container than chips, so I ordered large fries for all of us. We couldn't believe it when we opened the paper bag containing our meal.

Inside wasn't the three meagrely filled cardboard containers of chips we were expecting. It was as though they'd emptied a skip full of chips into our bag. I don't think we've ever seen so many chips. Maybe they'd given us six portions instead of three? We just about managed to polish off all these chips, along with our tasty burgers, and then we waddled slowly out of the restaurant to find the car.

Over the next few days, we told loads of people about the chip mountain we'd climbed at Five Guys. One or two friends messaged us back to say they'd been along to the new restaurant and had also faced a tsunami of fries.

It wasn't until I read Jay Baer's book that I found out this is deliberate. It's Five Guys' talk trigger. It's their special customer experience, designed specifically to create word of mouth. Whether you order small, regular or large fries they always give you a generous extra helping. It's why we were hip-deep in chips – we'd ordered the largest portions and Five Guys had added their signature extra on top.

So, when you're putting your activity together, let's think about what your special word-of-mouth feature could be. What will stand out? What will be memorable and get people talking? What will make them desperate to tell their friends and family?

Now you know the customer buying process you'll need to put together activity for each phase:

- How can you create awareness?
- How can you build interest and fuel desire?
- How can you encourage the customer to act?
- How can you keep the customer as a customer?
- How can you encourage the customer to become an advocate?

Let's have a look at the types of marketing activity available to us, then later we will put an activity plan together.

# Content

Content is activity primarily designed to answer the questions your customers will have about your offer.

For many people content marketing is a new thing, something they've only heard about over the last decade. The truth is it's been around for as long as marketing has existed.

We could consider content to be another type of communications activity, the same as advertising or a price promotion. Something that lasts for a brief time before we move on to the next communications campaign.

But customers will always have questions about your offer. And how you answer those questions is one of the ways your product or service is better and different from everyone else's. Content is evergreen, while advertising and promotions are short term. You could almost consider content to be part of your offer.

So, what is content compared to other forms of communication?

Traditional marketing communications interrupt. They're intrusive; they barge in and grab a potential customer by the scruff of the neck while shouting, "Buy my stuff." This might happen at a moment when such a blatant interruption is most unwelcome.

TV adverts interrupt the viewer's enjoyment of a show. You know what it's like. You're just getting to an exciting part of the narrative, or there's about to be a huge plot reveal, and then BANG, someone's talking to you about shampoo.

Of course, many people watch recordings of TV programmes and can use their remote controls to fast forward through the adverts, but avoiding the interruption is an interruption too. And I bet the advertisers hope you still see their brand and maybe even the call to action, even as you zap through at 12 times normal speed.

Billboard ads are similarly distracting. You're walking or driving along, you see a billboard ad and it distracts you. It makes you stop thinking about what was on your mind at the time and instead think about the product or service. Pop-up ads on computers butt in on your work and piss you off, although you can block them by installing a pop-up blocker, and printed adverts in newspapers and magazines mess with the flow of what you're reading.

Traditional communications have always been about getting the customer to stop what they're doing, stop what they're thinking about and drag their attention to the advertised product or service. Hopefully this will make them act, or at least remember a product or brand name.

Content, on the other hand, doesn't aim to interrupt. It doesn't smash its way in, screaming loudly. Content waits until the customer wants to consume it, on their terms and in their own time. Content is helpful. Content answers customers' questions.

As with all parts of the traditional marketing discipline, you can look on Google for a definition of content marketing and find a complete range of different answers. Some will be complex and unhelpful.

For the Offer–Goal–Activity marketing model, I'll use a definition of content I've been using with my clients for years:

Making stuff that teaches, entertains and inspires people to know, like and trust you enough to do business with you.

So, content doesn't interrupt and push product. Customers go looking for content, probably on Google, to answer questions they have about a problem. It teaches people things they might not have known about a market, about how a product or service solves a problem. What it does. How it does it. What its advantages are. What its disadvantages are. How it compares to everyone else's. How it's different and stands out from everyone else's. What it costs. How much it costs compared to everyone else's, and why.

It entertains. It might be funny, or it might use pop culture references (remember the zombie?) to make facts stick in the memory. It may be visually impressive. And it inspires. Hopefully, it makes the customer feel good about it and helps them decide they want to buy.

If you go to the trouble of researching your customer and understanding their problems and then put together a solution better and different to everyone else's, it makes sense to cover everything a customer might wonder about your offer and every question they might ask about it.

The answer to every question could be a blog article, a video, a podcast, an e-book or a webinar. It could even be a good old-fashioned printed article, booklet or glossy brochure.

But its aim is to teach, entertain and inspire. Not to interrupt. And not to enrage or annoy. (Remember the earlier examples of enraging marketing.) Great content is part of the reason you'll be better and different to everyone else.

So, how do you find out what people are asking about your product or service? We can go back to some of the research techniques we talked about earlier – or look at this remarkable website that can help you generate questions: https://answerthepublic.com.

Simply enter a keyword, topic or product name, or something related to your product, service or market, and it'll give you a stack of questions. I just tried putting in the word 'shampoo' and it returned 192 different questions about shampoo. That's 192 potential pieces of content you could put together – 192 blogs, videos, podcasts, webinars or booklets.

Okay, so some of the questions are probably not relevant. "Where did shampoo and pyjamas come from?" is one bizarre example. But most of its suggestions are solid. They are questions people will ask about shampoo.

Answerthepublic.com conveniently divides the questions into the following categories:

- How
- When
- Why
- Are
- What
- Will
- Where
- Which

- Who
- Can

When putting together content there are a couple of areas worth focusing on: comparisons and price. They're important because many businesses don't like to get into comparisons and price conversations.

People will have questions about the price of your products or services. Why hide it away in some difficult-to-find corner of your website? Why avoid talking about it in blogs and videos? Be open and honest about your prices. People will like you for it and it's another way you can create a connection with them. It's not a problem. Publish your prices and be proud.

Second, do comparisons with your competitors and other similar solutions. It's surprising how many companies shy away from this sort of content. Perhaps they don't want to draw their customers' attention to alternatives?

Remember, as we put together our Offer–Goal–Activity marketing plan we answered the question "How does it solve our customer's problem better and different than anyone else?"

If your customers are researching their options, they'll be on Google looking at alternatives anyway. You can't hide your competitors away by hoping your customers won't notice them or go looking for them. So, include all the comparison information your customers might want in your content. It's better they hear it from you rather than your competitors.

Once again, the answerthepublic.com website can help here by returning comparison ideas divided into the following categories:
- Versus
- Vs
- Like
- And
- Or

Once we've collected all these questions together, you can work on putting together content to answer them. The blogs, videos, audio and e-books will become part of your offer because they're helping your customers decide if they like and trust you, and whether they want to buy from you.

What you want to happen is that when someone types their question into Google or another search engine, it's your content that shows up in the search results. You can also use some paid advertising, perhaps on social media, to push more of your customers to your content. Let's compare the different types of content.

## Blogs

Blog is short for 'weblog' and is now a generic term for an article published on a website. In the early days of the internet, blogs were more personal, perhaps like online diaries for their authors. Now the blog section of company websites will have articles answering questions about their products and services with some 'human' stuff thrown in as well, for example, showing behind the scenes with their people. Once again, Problem–Agitate–Solution is a good formula to use when crafting a good blog post.

## Videos – pre-recorded and live

Producing videos used to be an expensive business. Now video is available to everyone through mobile devices and many people create high-quality videos and publish them on YouTube or Vimeo using little more than a mobile phone, a tripod and a decent microphone.

A vlog is a more personal showcase of an individual's business or lifestyle. Vloggers like Peter McKinnon, Casey Neistat and Kara & Nate have built massive followings sharing their lives on a daily basis.

You can use video to answer customer questions in two to three minute segments as well as longer and more in-depth productions.

Pre-recording a series of videos means you can edit out mistakes, but with live video available on most social media platforms such as

Facebook, Twitter, LinkedIn, YouTube and Instagram, and through streaming services like Twitch, many content creators are choosing to go live, warts and all, to the world. Live video can be extremely engaging and gives us the opportunity to answer questions in real time.

## Podcasts

A podcast is short for 'portable on demand broadcast'. It's a radio show you can download from a specific website or a mobile app such as Spotify. I'm a great fan of podcasts and my own Marketing & Finance Podcast has been successful and helped me promote myself as a marketing consultant and speaker. I was delighted to win the Best Podcast category in the 2019 Content Marketing Academy Awards.

The advantage of an audio podcast is people can listen to them anywhere: at home in the bath, at the gym on a treadmill, while commuting in a car, or on a train or aeroplane. Video is not always as accessible – we shouldn't be watching videos and driving!

And there's something intimate about a podcast. We're plugging the show's host, and their guests if they have them, into our earphones. It's an engaging experience.

## Webinars

A webinar is similar to attending a seminar or presentation except it's on a PC screen or mobile device. The presenter might use PowerPoint slides as they would at a conference. Sometimes we might be able to see the presenter, or we may just hear their voice synchronised with the slides.

Like a video production, content creators can broadcast a webinar live or pre-record the session and then have it run 'as live' at set times.

## Standing out

We must be aware there's a mass of content out there and we'll be competing with everyone else to grab our customers' attention.

Therefore, we must stand out and do something better and different to our competitors.

What could that be? It could be something as simple as the style of video – perhaps a fast-paced jump cut with sound effects. Or a podcast in the style of a game show. Standing out doesn't have to be wacky or annoying – although there's plenty of stuff out there that is. Just be yourself and have fun.

## Repurposing content

In addition to blogs, videos, audio and webinars, content takes many other forms. Email updates, white papers, newsletters and bulletins are just a few examples. One of the advantages of producing content is how you can repurpose it for different platforms.

For example, let's say you went live on Facebook and spent some time talking about your market and answering questions about why your products and services are better and different to everyone else's. You'll enjoy some exposure and customer engagement from the live broadcast.

You could edit the live broadcast into a shorter summary video, or simply leave the recording of the live video where your customers can watch it later at their leisure.

By getting a transcription of the video, you could produce a blog, again either edited or a complete reproduction. Depending on how long the video was, you could put together several blogs from such a transcript.

And by isolating the audio from the video source you could put together a podcast version as well.

Professional speakers will do a similar thing if they film themselves performing their keynote talk. They repurpose the video just as in the example above.

Repurposing is a powerful and cost-effective way of making content go further. You simply need to build it into your overall activity plan.

# Advertising

If you ask most non-marketers to define marketing, it's likely they'll say advertising.

Earlier in the book, I expressed an opinion that among the marketing profession the focus has switched too much to communication, of which advertising is, of course, a major part. And I lamented how we rarely hear about research, product development or pricing in marketing articles and at marketing conferences. This is a problem for the marketing profession, but it's totally understandable from a customer point of view.

Unless a customer has spent time in a focus group or been involved in product development, their main exposure to a company and its products will be through its communications, specifically its advertising. They won't have been through the process of setting a goal and coming up with an offer. They'll just see the activity, and advertising is likely to be part of that activity.

I make this distinction again to reinforce the importance of the Offer and Goal stages. Just because our customers view marketing as a communications process doesn't mean we should become seduced into thinking of it in this way too.

## What is advertising?

An advert is (usually) a paid-for communication designed to influence customers to take an action. This covers most product or service adverts that aim to get customers to open their wallets and hand over their cash and buy. Or take out their credit cards, type in their numbers and buy.

Most of these adverts interrupt the customer. A TV advert will interrupt their enjoyment of the show they're watching. A magazine advert will distract them from concentrating on the piece they're reading. You could consider a bottle of Diet Coke appearing in a movie scene as an advert too, even though it's not interrupting the film.

An advert can also be a paid-for communication designed to raise awareness of a company and its brand. This covers adverts about companies and their overall philosophies and aims. An advert for Nike the brand as opposed to one for Nike Free training shoes, for example. Or an advert for Coca Cola the brand as opposed to one for Diet Coke.

These adverts could also interrupt, but equally they could appear in the background and become almost subliminal. But it's advertising, just the same. Let's have a look at the various platforms for advertising.

## Broadcast media – TV and radio

TV offers perhaps the widest reach and can be the most expensive form of advertising. Even on local or specialist channels it can be difficult to target specific customer segments, so there'll always be some wastage.

Big corporates still spend billions of dollars a year on TV advertising, but some experts say it's a dying platform. With such high spending still going on, I'd argue it's hardly dying. It might be declining, but death is by no means certain.

Viewers use timeslip technology to fast forward through TV adverts, and some broadcast media services, such as Netflix, have no advertising at all. For these reasons, TV advertising is unlikely to be within reach of the budgets of smaller companies.

Radio, on the other hand, might fit a small company's budget much better because it's more cost-effective and the multitude of channels means targeting is easier. Unlike TV, people can't zap through the adverts (they may be driving) so the hit rate might be better.

## Printed media

A traditional marketing channel, printed media consists of magazines and newspapers. Magazines often specialise in narrow niches covering all sorts of industries, hobbies and pastimes. From luxury travel to food recipes, science fiction to cement mixers, fashion to gadgets, there's a magazine out there talking about it.

They'll often be glossy, with higher production values than newspapers, and they might be more visual, including more photography and colour.

Their specialism means targeting customers is easier. But magazines, especially high-circulation magazines, can also be expensive. And, depending upon their production schedule, you might have to send your advert weeks or months in advance – spontaneous promotions don't really work in magazines.

Newspapers, on the other hand, can be cheaper and cover local areas well, which again can be good for targeting customers. They're not as niche on subject matter as magazines and advert turnaround times are often a matter of days. The downside is the shelf life of a newspaper is shorter than a magazine – perhaps only one day, or a week at most. I remember one boss of mine saying, "Today's newspapers are tomorrow's chip wrappers."

Printed media circulations are generally on the decline, and often people go to the equivalent magazine or newspaper website instead. Pop-up adverts on newspaper and magazine websites are among the most annoying and intrusive of them all, with video windows popping up as you scroll down the page, often blocking the text you're trying to read. As soon as you've aimed your cursor at the little cross to zap the advert, another one zips in to take its place. It's almost like a modern version of the arcade game Space Invaders. Wave upon wave of unstoppable, enraging adverts.

## Other media

Other options for adverts include billboards, bus stops, the sides of buses, the back of the seats on planes, inside taxis and any other place where customers might see them.

In Edinburgh, halfway down the famous Waverley Steps to the

city's railway station, there's a small shop specialising in fixing mobile phone screens. At the top of the steps is the Apple Store. The specialist shop often has a man carrying a gigantic sign offering *much cheaper phone screen repairs than the Apple Store* with an arrow pointing across the road. It makes me chuckle every time I see it.

It's worth getting out and about to see what local businesses are doing with their marketing activity. It's tempting always to look at global brands like Apple, Nike, Starbucks and British Airways. But you might find more inspiration from the Renroc Café in Edinburgh, LifeSearch in the UK or the Represent Agency in Belgrade.

Some outside advertising spaces like billboards and bus stops now have digital screens and often rotate different adverts rather than the static versions of old.

## Direct marketing

This is a form of advertising targeted at individuals. Direct mail, often referred to as junk mail by customers, can range from simple leaflets stuffed through letter boxes by local plumbers or takeaway restaurants to elaborate and glossy packages including many foldout elements, booklets and other material.

As a marketer, I used to open every item of junk mail, whether advertising the latest BMW 3 Series, an over-50s life insurance policy or a luxury holiday in the Caribbean. Always curious about the wording and the layout, I'd read them, but I can't recall ever buying from them. But some people did, and for a time direct mail worked. I rarely get direct mail except from credit card companies.

That said, the direct mail I do respond to tends to be the leaflets dropped by local tradesmen, especially the one offering to clear autumn leaves out of the guttering on our house.

Email is a form of direct marketing and comes without the prohibitive costs associated with producing glossy mail packs and paying for postage. All you need is a good email service provider, like Aweber or MailChimp, and you can start to build a list of potential customers.

One of the most common tactics is to offer a free piece of content, referred to by the jargon term *lead magnet,* in exchange for the potential customer giving you their email address. Once they are on your list, tactics include sending the customer email newsletters, relevant tips and tricks and, of course, invitations to buy products and services.

Since May 2018 and the introduction of the European GDPR rules the regulations around building lists are much tougher and you must ensure you have permission to email your clients and that they wilfully agreed to be on your list.

Telephone marketing is another form of direct marketing. How many phone calls have you received from companies offering double glazing or new kitchens? And then there are the annoying calls from legal companies asking you if you've recently been in a car accident so they can help you claim compensation. There are many telesales companies that I know are legitimate, sell good products and respect the people they call, but there are others who I believe lack any integrity at all. People call them 'ambulance chasers'.

## Internet

Banner ads and pop-up ads on webpages are common forms of internet advertising. In the background, complex 'programmatic' algorithms dictate how companies bid for the time and space for their adverts to appear. This 'programmatic' advertising is highly targeted and driven by complex algorithms, but I guess someone must click through and end up buying. By 2019, programmatic advertising spend will reach US $45.72 billion[7], having grown more than two and a half times over just four years.

Personally, I find internet adverts the most intrusive and annoying of all. Even if you use browser pop-up ad blockers, many seem to be

---

7 https://www.acuityads.com/blog/2017/12/15/what-is-programmatic-advertising/ (accessed Jan 2020)

able to get around them. I mentioned before how some magazine and newspaper websites bombard you with pop-up videos that appear every time you scroll down a page. It's intrusive marketing at its worst. And it may be beyond the budgets of smaller businesses.

You can use Google Ads (formerly Google AdWords) to try to get your internet adverts onto relevant websites. An alternative is a paid search, where you bid a 'cost per click' amount to get your advert onto a search results page so you appear when someone is searching for a specific term.

## Social media

When Facebook first hit the web and *Twitter* came along soon after, marketers who understood it were jumping for joy. Here was a series of platforms offering them almost free access to millions of people. Although meant to be a two-way conversation where people could share photos and experiences, marketers quickly realised they could use social media as just another form of broadcast media: just another billboard. For a fleeting moment they got away with posts that were just free adverts.

Now algorithms as complex as the programmatic algorithms carefully select what most people see on social media. And overall, if you want to push products or services, or if you want to sell stuff, then you're going to have to pay to get in front of more people. This isn't a bad thing and it's true to say Facebook, Twitter and Instagram advertising can be highly effective.

Social media advertising can be cost-effective for small companies and entrepreneurs. Back in the 'Who is your customer?' section we looked at how specific Facebook allows you to be when setting up a target audience.

We can make our adverts feel less intrusive on Facebook by closely targeting them to what people are looking at. I'm sure this has happened to you. You're browsing the internet – let's say you're looking at hotels for an upcoming holiday. Someone's told you to have a look at Galley Bay, a hotel in Antigua.

You look at a few pages on the Galley Bay website, noting the gorgeous beach and the accommodation set in lush green gardens. You might bookmark the site. Later, your mouse pointer guides you back to check your Facebook page, and what happens? There's an advert for Galley Bay in your Facebook feed.

And it's not an intrusive, annoying advert either. It may build upon some of the information you found on the website. Or it talks more about the facilities, or perhaps offers you an early booking discount. Unlike irrelevant adverts that interrupt your TV show or pop up while you're trying to read a blog article, you almost don't mind these adverts. You almost expect them.

Unless you know what's going on, this might feel a little like magic. What happens when you visit the Galley Bay website is a piece of code called a Facebook pixel, a bit like a cookie, records your visit. Galley Bay can then set up a target audience on Facebook that consists of people who've browsed their website. It's that easy.

## Advertising content

Before the rise of internet, advertising served to raise awareness of brands, products and services.

With content now forming such an important part of marketing activity we're seeing more advertising, particularly on social media, focused on guiding customers to useful content that answers the questions they have on our offers.

My friend and Facebook Ads expert Gavin Bell has a straightforward process for helping his clients increase their sales using Facebook. It's a combination of content and advertising.

Imagine Debbie is a chef specialising in cooking low fat and healthy meals. Her goal is to sell her £599 online cookery course. Gavin says the first stage is for Debbie to put together some free content. Let's imagine she records a series of videos for her YouTube channel where she cooks one of her recipes. Using clever editing, she makes a meal that takes 30 minutes to prepare in real time, in just over three minutes.

At the end of her video she invites viewers to visit her website and download a free recipe sheet. Some viewers follow her call to action and get the PDF by typing their email in the box.

Debbie has set up a Facebook pixel to record people visiting her site and can then use a Facebook Ads campaign to draw their attention to the cookery course.

She could set up a target audience of people who've simply visited her site, or people who've subscribed to her email list by downloading the recipe.

People who've watched her YouTube videos and downloaded her recipe sheet will be more engaged by her Facebook adverts because they won't feel as intrusive as those that interrupt elsewhere and perhaps promote products and services that aren't relevant to them.

# How to put together content, advertising and promotions

A quick search on Google brings up hundreds of articles on promotion formulas, advert templates and sales copywriting styles. Some are great and have led to high levels of sales, so it's worth having a read through them. Take some notes and maybe have a go at coming up with some draft adverts yourself.

Many of these formulas and templates are, however, simply variations on two we've discussed in the book already:

Attract–Interest–Desire–Action (AIDA) and Problem–Agitate–Solution (PAS).

As a rule, use the AIDA formula for adverts and the PAS formula for sales pages or communications once the customer has started to interact with you.

For example, you might put together a Facebook advert using the AIDA formula. This could be a provocative headline or image designed to grab the customer's attention.

Once a customer has found your website, sales pages or product and service information you already have their attention and want them to buy. At this stage the PAS formula might work better.

Sometimes the method of attracting the customer's attention is by making them think about a problem, so the two formulas can work together.

*"Fed up with dull dry hair?"* or a variation of this statement has appeared in many adverts and sales pages for shampoo. Here the copywriter has used a problem to grab the attention of the customer.

"Sucks, doesn't it? Especially as you have an important presentation to do next week when you want to look immaculate." Now the copywriter is agitating the problem.

Hopefully these 'problem' and 'agitate' statements will resonate with the customer and they'll now be receptive to the solution:

"Our shampoo penetrates deep into your hair follicles and hydrates from the inside, making your hair dazzle with a shiny glow."

Unless you are an advertising or sales copy expert, my advice is to get help. Writing advertising and sales copy is a special skill. There are experts out there who have spent years honing their craft and can command high fees for simply putting together a sales email. You can find agencies specialising in just this sort of copy preparation and, of course, you can probably find someone on Fiverr who'll write an advert for you for a fiver. But will it be any good?

Once we move beyond words and start thinking about video or audio adverts and sales content, then we need to tap into a wider set of skills.

AIDA and PAS still work as a basic framework for adverts and sales content whether these are written sales pages, audio or full video productions.

But the more we move to producing an advert or sales content involving other digital media, the more important it becomes to call in the experts – a creative agency, for example. And that's going to mean investment.

Of course, it's possible to produce your own adverts and sales content using video or audio, and some small companies manage this well. Some have even set up their own in-house production teams and if that's possible then it's the way to go. But sometimes it's better to outsource to an agency.

When you do this it's important to let them do their job, which is to create an advert or some sales content that brings in customers, makes sales and grows your business. But let them do what they do best – being creative.

I've worked with many agencies over the years and I've put together newspaper adverts, billboard adverts, video adverts and audio sales content. During the projects the people running the creative agencies have become friends. And the one thing they all say is a problem is the quality of the brief from their clients.

Quite often the client will not have gone through the Offer and

Goal part of their marketing plan. They'll simply come along and say, "We want an advert for our product. And we have an idea for some lovely cliff top shots in the video."

So, the agency starts having to fill in the blanks and trying to guess what the offer and goals are. Without a strong brief, the final execution of the advert either won't work or it will be a disappointment to the client.

I experienced this early on in my career when I was a senior marketing assistant. We'd put together a brief for a series of magazine and billboard adverts and asked three agencies to pitch their ideas based on our brief.

A few weeks later, we blocked out the entire day and invited each of the agencies to present their concepts to us. I always enjoyed these pitch meetings with the concept boards and the visuals. I found it exciting. But on this occasion, as the three agencies revealed their concepts, I couldn't help feeling disappointed. The adverts didn't hit the spot for me. The visuals didn't feel right, and nothing made me want to punch the air and scream, "*YES!*"

Once the three agencies had left, we sat in the meeting room and held a debrief. The marketing director said, "It's not the agencies' fault. It was our brief. We didn't give them a strategy, so they tried to fill in the gaps themselves and they failed."

When briefing an agency, it's vital to tell them the goal – is it a certain amount of sales or an increase in market share? – and they need to know about the offer.

They need to know who the customer is, what their problem is, what your solution to the problem is, and why it's better and different than everyone else's. If they have all the information, the agency can focus on what it does best: the creativity and the execution.

It's when they haven't got all the information that problems appear. They start trying to fill in those blanks themselves and the creative execution suffers as a result.

Here's an example from popular culture.

The UK TV show *The Apprentice* features 14 entrepreneurs hoping to become the business partner of Lord Alan Sugar, the multi-millionaire founder of many businesses, including Amstrad. Each week they must complete business-related tasks, after which there is a tense boardroom grilling and one or more people in the losing team gets fired by Lord Sugar.

Each year, one of the episodes is all about putting together an advertising campaign for a specific product. In the 2018 series Lord Sugar asked the candidates to put together an advertising campaign for a low-cost airline. The advertising episode is my favourite every season and I love it and hate it in equal measure.

But on each occasion the candidates make the fundamental error of not having a goal and an offer and therefore not briefing the creatives properly. And the resulting adverts, whether they're for digital billboards or TV, fail spectacularly. Often, they're downright embarrassing.

This year, one of the candidates tried to come up with a logo for the low-cost airline. He sketched out his ideas on a piece of paper and then took it along to the creative agency. The conversation went something like this.

"Here's my rough drawing of a logo for the airline. Can you make it look professional?"

The designer looks at the scribbled logo and we can see her wincing. "Sure," she replies with a forced smile. But we know what she's really thinking. She's really thinking the idea for the logo is rubbish and she's feeling genuine pain about putting together a professional-looking version of the rubbish idea.

It's the same with the adverts and the digital billboards. The candidates have an idea for a video or a digital billboard, for example, "I want a man and woman walking along a beach, drinking a large gin and tonic," and they just tell the creatives to "make it". The ideas are usually awful. The creatives try their hardest to polish the turd, to put lipstick on the pig. But they fail. Why?

Because the candidates haven't briefed them properly to allow them to do their creative jobs. The candidates are not the creatives. Apart from the odd one who might have design skills, they don't have the skills to come up with clever ideas for adverts. But they don't let the creatives create.

The way they should work with the creatives is to tell them what their goal is (in this example to sell airline seats). They need to tell them about their offer, specify who their target market is and what problems the target market has and outline how their low-cost airline solves the problem better and different than everyone else. Armed with this information, the creatives can get on with their job as creators.

If they went through this process, then the adverts presented to Lord Sugar might be engaging and effective. They might follow the AIDA or the PAS format and so appeal to their target market. And they might get people to act.

Throughout this book my key message has been that marketing is not just about communications. It's also about the offer and the goals. And the offer comes from a deep, almost obsessive understanding of the customer. If you have the goals and the offer nailed, then you are in a strong position to brief someone to put together great activity for you – content, communications and promotions that engage your customers.

Without an offer and a goal, you'll end up with a disappointing set of activities – disappointing in execution and disappointing in their ability to generate sales.

You can use the Offer–Goal–Activity model to write an agency brief to avoid the embarrassing situations the apprentices get themselves into.

# Price promotions

Running price promotions can be one of the most effective types of marketing activity. People love a bargain – it's why stores run sales. We see winter sales, Boxing Day sales and Black Friday sales.

The public's insatiable love of the Boxing Day sale baffles me. Christmas trees appear in shops in the middle of September and the sound of Noddy Holder from Slade singing "Merry Christmas, Everyone!" wafts out of the stores as soon as the doors slide open. High street brands and the media ram Christmas messages down our throats for nearly four months.

And yet, after four months of non-stop shopping and spending and preparing for Christmas Day, some people have just one day off to guzzle their wine and devour their turkey and then they're back out on Boxing Day, waiting in line in the early hours for even more shopping.

I'm usually tucked up in bed nursing a thick head and a bloated belly and want nothing more than to spend the day chilling in front of the TV, eating turkey leftovers. The behaviour might baffle me, but I understand the power of price in driving the customer to seek out a bargain.

Back in the chapter on offer, you worked out what your base price should be. You don't want to lose money and you should try to cover your costs, ideally making a profit. But there will be times when it makes business sense to lower the price to get more customers through the door.

Beware of being a loss leader or driving yourself down a low-cost route. Also be aware of the differences in pricing a product or a service. It's easier to run a price promotion on a product like a vacuum cleaner, a place at a conference, a course or a mattress.

If you're offering a service, such as consultancy or coaching, be careful about offering discounts. If you've built up many years of experience in your industry, then you'll bring your customer more value than simply the time you spend with them. And you need to build that value into the price you charge.

When I think about whether I should offer a discount on consultancy services, I default to my reaction when potential customers ask for a discount. I'll say, "It wouldn't be fair on my clients who have paid my rates, and are happy to pay my rates, if I offered you a lower price."

For products, discounts can be an effective way of bringing in new customers, but they can also cause customers to only buy from you when you're running a price promotion. You know your customers and who you're targeting, and therefore you know what price they can support.

Messing about with prices can bring in more customers, but prices can also affect how much customers trust your business.

I've already mentioned the practice of many insurance companies charging new customers cheaper premiums while fleecing their existing customers to keep profits up. Before the internet, companies could hide these dodgy practices behind big corporate boardroom doors. Now they can no longer pull the wool over their customers' eyes. They can find out what companies are up to with a quick Google search.

What you do with your prices can give the customer an idea about your integrity as a business. For some brands, the price discount is a permanent part of the offer. DFS, the sofa manufacturer and retailer, is always running sales. And they keep using scarcity tactics to get people through the doors.

The DFS sale finishes on Saturday.

And the reason it finishes on Saturday is because the next one starts on Sunday. People recognise DFS's pricing activity for what it is. Just part of the offer. Most probably realise what's going on and we might have a laugh about it in the pub. It's even found its way into popular culture.

Scarcity as part of a price promotion can be even more powerful. Conferences are good at this. They'll launch some early bird tickets, the cheapest they have available, and they'll communicate aggressively how many they have left or on which date they stop being available. They'll then release the next tier of tickets and use similar scarcity messages to boost sales of that tier.

It's effective, but businesses can abuse scarcity.

How many adverts have you seen where the brand says the price of the course or an event will go up after a specific date? Then after the date they contact you again and say they have extended the deadline. And they keep extending the deadline. Is this not just another legitimate way of playing the scarcity card? To me, it's disingenuous. Having an early bird ticket promotion, sticking to your guns and putting the price up feels like a well-thought-through strategy, and the conference is telling the truth.

Using scarcity and not following through on it feels more manipulative. It's an outright lie. Would you trust a company that lies? Customers want to trust the companies they deal with, and the latter behaviour erodes trust.

Here are four tips for successful price promotions.

## Don't be predictable

Everyone expects Black Friday and Boxing Day sales, and it's tempting to join the masses and offer price reductions too. But if everyone is discounting at the same time then it's harder to stand out, so you must make your marketing activity even more effective to rise above all the other deals. Why not run your promotions at a different time? Become known as the company in your space who moved Boxing Day to March?

It's also tempting to link price promotions to 'national' marketing days. Pretty much every day of the year is a 'national something' day: National Love Your Pets Day, National No Smoking Day, National Gardening Day. These sit alongside the more established Mother's Day, Father's Day, and Valentine's Day. Again, it's tempting to link a price promotion (or marketing communication) to these events, but many other companies will be thinking the same thing. Stand out and think differently.

## Keep the promotion period short

Unless you want to bake an almost permanent discount into your offer like DFS sofas, try to keep your price promotions short and play on the scarcity.

In the UK, the price promotion activity of supermarket brands like Tesco and Sainsbury's have been made less powerful by the constant low-price approach of Aldi and Lidl. If you train your customers to expect frequent and long price promotions, they'll get used to them, and you'll find yourself becoming low-cost full time because customers move on when you aren't discounting.

So, try price promotions for short periods and less often, and try to avoid following the lead of your competitors. Let your promotions be a surprise for your customers.

## Have clear rules and stick to them

The conference early bird ticket model is legitimate and trustworthy. Telling customers they have until the end of the month to buy up to 100 tickets at 60% of the full price will create a scarcity nudge that might make them take action and buy before the deadline. At the end of the month, put the price up to the next tier and keep it there until the next deadline.

Don't extend the deadline you've already set because it will lessen the scarcity effect and may introduce an element of distrust. And don't offer bigger discounts closer to the date of the conference, offering people better deals than for those who did part with their cash early. It's a sure-fire way to annoy customers and destroy trust.

## Break even

Always cover your costs. Break even. Never discount prices so much that you're losing money.

# Publicity and PR

The next item in our marketing activity toolbox is publicity, which is often confused with public relations.

Publicity is, in fact, a part of public relations and involves getting mentions of your business, brand, people, products and services in media publications online and in print. This could simply be a printed quote such as

Jenny Smith, head of marketing at Cool Cupcakes said, "With our customers flavour comes first, followed by how our cakes look. They love vibrant colours."

That's publicity. If you are a fitness expert and speak to a journalist from the Daily Mail who's drafting an article about fad diets and she quotes you in the article, that's publicity. If you have a good relationship with a media company and they ask you to write an article for them, or shoot a video or record an audio, that's publicity. Or if you become particularly well-known in a specific industry or an expert in a certain topic, they may ask you to appear on TV or radio or shoot video or record audio for a website feature.

Public relations is wider than just publicity. It's also about creating relationships with other organisations, possibly including the government, so the discipline goes beyond just trying to secure coverage.

PR manages the public image of your brand, and they'll need to step in if something goes wrong and you generate bad publicity for your brand. Remember when I appeared on TV to defend my company when they turned down an insurance claim? The PR team helped get us through the crisis.

Local and national newspapers, trade publications, general magazines, specialist magazines and all their associated websites are constantly looking for stories. If you work on building a relationship with the media in your area of expertise, they may start quoting you quite often. And you might even find them asking you to write placed articles or create other content.

In this digital world you no longer need to confine yourself to traditional news or lifestyle publications where journalists put together the content. You can look beyond them to relevant blog sites, podcasts and video shows. You may want to talk to influencers — those who have a strong following and influence on social media platforms. Whatever niche you've found for yourself there'll undoubtedly be plenty of media you can approach, either to try to get quoted or to produce content for them. Writing a guest post on a blog is one example.

But there are rules. The media is not a free advertising platform and most journalists are not there to promote your company or its products. They have news stories to write and opinions to collect. If they think you're after some free advertising they'll cut any conversation short.

If you send them a press release about a special deal you're doing on coffee in your cafe, they're unlikely to write about it. Give them a story about how you went to Colombia to talk to Fairtrade representatives about your new flavour line and they might be interested in running it.

I learned about the power of PR early in my career. After I moved to Edinburgh the company wanted to put me forward as a spokesperson for the brand. I flew down to London to meet with the PR agency and they introduced me to a gentleman who would shape my publicity skills. I hit it off with Terry Hepplewhite straight away. Not only was he an expert in PR and publicity, he also liked all the same prog rock and heavy metal bands I did. We often shared many a beer talking about Genesis, Jethro Tull and Magnum.

Terry gave me three rules for building relationships with journalists and they're just as relevant now as they were 20 years ago.

- Always give the journalist a real story and not just the corporate spin about your product or service.
- If you say you're going to phone back, do it. Quickly.
- Never say no to a placed article.

Sticking to those rules, within a couple of years I became one of the most quoted spokespeople in my industry. One day I met one of my peers from a competitor company. We started talking about PR and he said, "Off the record, we're really jealous about the amount of publicity you get for your company. What do you do to get all these publications to quote you so much? And how do you get asked to write so many articles?"

I turned it back on him and asked him what their tactics were. He said, "We tend to invite the journalists into the office and the high-ups meet them in the boardroom and we'll go through our press release or a few PowerPoint slides."

I saw two problems at once. They weren't giving the journalists a real story and they weren't building a relationship. It was all corporate spin. I told him what I did instead. I usually took the journalists out for a coffee, or a beer or glass of wine, and we talked about normal stuff. Holidays. Music. Interests. Then I'd slip in the real story, embellished with facts about the product or service. It was more about the relationship than the messages.

One of the most effective ways of getting a journalist to remember me was the good old-fashioned business card. This wouldn't work today because so few of us use business cards anymore, but at the time it was simple and effective.

At the end of the meeting I'd pull out a business card. On the back, as they watched, I'd draw a cartoon and a couple of words to remind them of the real story we'd talked about. Everyone in my industry would give out a business card to a journalist after a meeting, but I was the only one who drew a cartoon on the back. This gesture, as small as it was, made me stand out. Journalists remembered me. And when they were looking for a quote, or a story, or someone to write an article, I'd be at the top of the list.

At the start of my second full year working with Terry, I wrote a PR strategy for my brand and sent it to him so we could plan activity any meetings for the year ahead. He phoned me up and said, "This is fantastic. And it's also the first time someone in a position like yours has written a strategy like this without being bullied into it by us."

*Money Marketing* magazine ran an interview with Terry a few years later, and he mentioned me as being "a PR's dream. He always has a story and always phones back."

Of course, when I started working with Terry, the internet was only just getting going. We were dealing mainly with printed media. In the digital age, it's much harder to get a journalist out to have a coffee or a beer or glass of wine. Skype or Messenger or Twitter are much more economical for a time-poor journalist when their editors are on their back chasing deadlines. But the principles still apply. It's still about the real story.

The good old-fashioned press release is the favoured communications vehicle for journalists, and you can find many press release templates on the internet telling you how to structure a good one. But conforming to the norm isn't necessarily the best way to stand out. Don't forget a journalist's inbox is likely to be chock-full of press releases every day.

I subscribe to several PR wires because I'm curious about the messages companies are putting out there. It's rare any of the press releases I receive make me want to read beyond the heading.

Journalists aren't going to open all of them or even read many of them. An intriguing headline and opening paragraph might catch their attention, but they're not interested in your new product or service, or slight tweak to it. And they're not there to help you promote it. But give them a real story with which your product or service is associated, and you may make them read further, maybe even enough to pick up the phone.

I abandoned formal press release templates years ago in favour of simple emails with a powerful headline, interesting story and believable link to my product or service. This approach worked and I never got any bad feedback from journalists for not sending a formal press release. I never put the words 'press release' in the heading and I never used the term -ENDS- at the end.

I asked a friend of mine what -ENDS- was all about and he said it was to separate the main section of the press release from the section headed Notes for Editors. Isn't a heading called Notes for Editors enough to create the separation? -ENDS- is a hangover from the days of telegrams, surely?

Journalists won't be impressed with words like 'innovative' and 'revolutionary' in press releases. They'll know a service claiming to be 'world class' probably won't be. Clichés don't work.

When I've worked with consultancy customers on PR projects, I've avoided such weasel language. My preferred approach is:

Our product/service stands out because: followed by a list of facts backed by proof.

Creating content for the media is another way to get coverage for your brand, product or service. When I started in marketing this would have been a written article, but now publications might also be looking for video and audio content.

If you want to target a specific title it pays to work on building a relationship with the publication first. What's their focus? What's their style of article like? What's the average length of features? Never pitch an idea to an editor without doing some homework on the publication first, and maybe spend time developing a relationship with the editor or journalist before you go into pitch mode. Follow them on Twitter, engage them in conversation and share some of their articles.

On Twitter you can look at the hashtag #JournoRequest to find the sort of questions journalists are asking and the stories they're writing. Use the search techniques I described earlier to narrow the search to your area of expertise, and there you have the beginnings of a connection.

Then pitch them your idea, again based around a real story. Don't include any self-promotion or hard sell (they'll edit it out if they don't reject the piece first). You might make a reference to your brand product or service if the context is right. But, overall, you'll be giving them the piece to help increase your profile and establish or boost your expertise in the sector.

Earlier in the book I mentioned my good friend Neil Cameron, a

PR expert I worked with in big corporate. He was great at finding stories related to our products and generating publicity. For example, he'd run a small research project asking customers about a topic related to our products. He built in a general set of questions, some focusing on UK regions. With his research data he pitched the story to UK regional radio stations, which love region-specific data. We'd then spend the day in a recording studio phoning into the radio stations and appearing on a whole host of shows to talk about our research.

When we talked to the journalist from the Yorkshire region, we could say something like, "While 20% of people in the UK said they worried about their health every day, in Yorkshire it was surprisingly higher, at 32%."

Sometimes we'd do between 15 and 20 interviews in a day. I'd often have to go to Boots the Chemist and buy some throat lozenges to keep me going. These 'radio days' were such an effective way of getting publicity for our company and its products.

PR is not my specialty, but I've led some successful PR campaigns and even managed PR for consultancy clients. It's a cost-effective and powerful way to get your message out there. I've only just scratched the surface in this chapter and would encourage you to read more on the topic.

Terry's rules, adapted for the digital world, still work for me today.

- Always give the journalist (or blogger) a real story and not just the corporate spin about your product and service.
- If you say you're going to phone, message, tweet or Skype back, do it. Quickly.
- Never say no to a placed article, blog, video or audio.

# Sales and marketing working together

If your company is big enough to have both a marketing team and a sales team, it's essential they work together to meet your business goals.

They perform different roles in the customer buying process, but they complement each other perfectly.

If you're a smaller company, with perhaps one or two people combining marketing and sales work, it's still important to know the differences and to understand how the functions dovetail.

Sadly, in many larger organisations, sales and marketing are often at loggerheads. There's an unhealthy tension. Perhaps even some animosity. In my experience, this almost always comes from a lack of understanding on behalf of both teams of what each does and who's responsible for what. I've found it's also due to the fact they haven't worked together from the start: working out who the customer is, what their problems are and how they solve those problems better and different to anyone else.

When I moved up to Edinburgh a quarter of a lifetime ago, to join Steeple Fingers and his team, I discovered at once there was a poor relationship between sales and marketing.

It didn't help that the sales director lived and worked at the other end of the country. In the days before video conferencing, this meant a series of terse phone calls and emails were the only means of communication.

I found the sales team constantly moaning about how marketing wasn't giving them the right tools to help them sell the company's products and services. And the marketing team were constantly moaning that sales weren't using the promotional material they'd put together and didn't 'get' the key messages.

The marketing director disliked the sales director, saying the latter drank like a fish and played too much golf. The sales director disliked the marketing director, saying he thought the latter didn't play enough golf and *looked* like a fish.

Perhaps because I was new, and didn't have an existing reputation within the organisation, I found it easy to get on with both teams. After sharing gallons of coffee and beer, and some solid rounds of golf, I understood what the problems were. Each team did its own thing because they weren't bound together by a shared understanding.

I spent much of my time talking to the salespeople and trying to bridge the gap. We let the directors continue with their feud whilst we started to work together at the coalface. Soon I was out doing presentations with the sales team and they started to use the marketing material I put together.

Several years went by until one day the sales director acknowledged that I had effectively become the 'AND' in sales and marketing. On several occasions, he helped me to drink like a fish too.

Before the internet and digital developed, the roles of sales and marketing were, perhaps, more distinct than they are now.

Marketing would identify the customer, find out what their problems were, design products and services to fix those problems and then produce communications material to catch the customers' attention and build awareness of those products and services.

Sales would follow up on the awareness created by the marketing activity, answer customer questions, overcome any objections and close the sale.

For the relationship to work the marketing team would not only have to put together the promotional communications, but also material the sales team could use to answer the customers' questions. Product guides, brochures and other collateral.

Before the internet and Google, it was usually the sales team that answered questions customers had about the products, how they solved their problems, and why they were better and different to anyone else's.

In the modern digital world, we know, thanks to Google's Zero Moment of Truth, that 70% of buying decisions now start with a

Google search. Marketing is still responsible for raising awareness through advertising and promotions, but customers are now Googling their questions and finding answers through content.

It's a subtle but crucial difference. Customers can now get answers to their questions before they contact the company for the first time. The sales team still need to close the deal, but it's likely they won't have as many questions to answer as they had in the past. And if the customer does have questions then the sales team can refer them to the content that answers them.

In the old world, sales and marketing clashed if they didn't work through the Offer-Goal-Activity model (or whatever strategic process existed in the company) together, right from the start.

In the new digital world, it's the same. Unless both teams work together on planning the Offer-Goal-Activity, then they'll clash. And as the sales team are still going to be answering questions (even if the customer can find out answers more easily now), they have to be involved in defining the questions that get turned into videos and articles answering those questions.

Working together, the marketing and sales teams can then weave the content into the sales process.

Imagine a member of the sales team is setting up appointments to follow up on leads. In the confirmation email they could say, "Looking forward to seeing you on Friday. I know you'll want to talk about how our product can meet your requirements better and different to everyone else, so here's a link to a couple of short videos that answer that question."

Or if a customer asks a specific question in advance of the meeting then the salesperson can again email or message the link to the video or article answering the question.

Say at the meeting the customer asks a question about the price of the product, the salesperson can answer the question and then immediately follow up with an email or message pointing to another video or article confirming the answer given.

The links to content create a fine web of information designed to help the customer build enough trust in the company to make a decision to buy.

If sales and marketing work together in this way, both teams will have a thorough understanding of the offer, and they'll have agreed on the activity they need to make the buying process easy and smooth for the customer.

I still consult for organisations where there is an unhealthy relationship between sales and marketing. The answer is always to get the teams working together through the Offer-Goal-Activity model to develop a shared understanding, and weave great content into the buying process so customers can find answers or the sales team can refer them to those answers.

This is how you become the 'AND' in sales and marketing.

# Putting the activity plan together

Now you've decided on the marketing activity to promote your offer and meet your goals, it's important to put everything into a plan.

I said earlier my two main weaknesses in business are 'sums' and the detail of planning. I've always made sure I compensate for these weaknesses by hiring a good accountant and finding someone to help me with planning. If you're a one-person company this might mean outsourcing this work. If you run a small or medium sized company, then obviously you can employ an expert to help.

My memories of planning in big corporate involve a haze of Excel spreadsheets and Gantt charts and I guess these are still fine. But now there is so much software and so many apps out there that planning needn't be as scary. Modern software and apps are easy to use and have great interfaces. From full content management systems to apps like Trello, you'll find something to meet your needs.

The bottom line is finding something that lets you put together a plan everyone can follow and understand, especially any salespeople you want to make sure are aligned with your marketing efforts.

As I'm not a planning expert I don't have a tried and trusted template for setting out an activity plan and schedule, but I do like to split marketing activity into five sections:

- Content
- Content advertising
- Product/service/brand advertising
- Price promotions
- PR

As I said earlier, your content is likely to be a long-term commitment rather than a short-term campaign. It's almost part of your offer. It lets your customers find answers to the questions they might have about your offer. And your salespeople can use the same content to answer customer questions when they are further along in the buying process.

# Content

Armed with your list of questions compiled using the *answerthepublic* website and, more importantly, from your own sales and customer service people if you have them, set up a plan for putting together and publishing content that answers these questions; videos, blogs and eBooks.

Let's take a video as an example. Create a calendar and set a date against each of the following stages for each piece of content.

- Produce Video Q1 (script, shoot, edit)
- Sign off Video Q1
- Publish Video Q1 (upload to YouTube or Vimeo and embed back into your website)
- Organic social media promotion on platforms relevant to your customers (this could be a recurring activity)
- Supply links to salespeople to include in their communications

If you're going to repurpose the video, then also create dates in the calendar for those items, for example: create an audio version of Video Q1, get a transcript of the video and edit it as a blog, make short snippets of the video and audio for social media teasers.

## Content advertising

When social media platforms first appeared in the late 2000s marketers rubbed their hands together with glee, for here was a free advertising platform. For a while it worked, but once established, the social media platforms started to use their algorithms to limit the number of people seeing each post in their feeds. Now an organic post will have a limited reach and the only way to get in front of more people is to pay.

Again, create a calendar and set a date against each of the following stages.

- Create advert with call to action to watch Video Q1

- Sign off advert
- Set up advert on relevant platform (probably social media but could be other digital advertising route) with start date and end date

## Product/service/brand advertising

Whilst publishing content to support your offer is an ongoing 'evergreen' activity, product/service/brand advertising is likely to be more campaign driven, lasting for a brief period.

If you're working with an agency, you'll be able to brief them well because you've put together your offer and goals. Your one-liner and benefit statements might appear in these communications.

- Create a calendar and set a date against each of the following stages:
- Brief agency
- Produce advertising campaign for desired platform(s)
- Sign off campaign
- Start date
- End date
- Communicate full details of campaign with salespeople (who'll have been involved right from the start anyway, right?)

## Price promotions

When you were putting together your offer you answered the question, "What's the minimum you must charge for this to make a profit?" Ideally, you don't want to go below this base price but sometimes it might be worth running a price promotion.

Again, create a calendar and set a date against each of the following stages:

- Define price promotion (discount, coupons, early bird)

- Sign off
- Start date
- End date
- Communicate full details of campaign with salespeople

Of course, you'll most likely put together some content about the price promotion, with associated content advertising, or general advertising as well, so put these in the plan as well.

## PR

Finally, include any public relations activity in the plan. This could include press releases about product or service launches, significant content or promotional campaigns, and any placed articles, blogs, videos or audios.

- For press releases, set a date against each of the following stages:
- Draft press release
- Sign off
- Issue to selected media outlets
- For placed articles, blogs, videos or audios, set a date against each of the following stages:
- Agree brief from media outlet
- Produce content
- Sign off
- Agree publishing date with media outlet
- Put together organic social media activity to draw attention to the placed content

On reading back through this list, I shudder a little, but that's my weakness as a planner grabbing hold. Get someone to do this for you and you'll increase your chance of success. And you'll have a document that summarises all your activity so everyone in the company knows what's happening and when.

# Let's go back to brand for a moment

The Offer–Goal–Activity marketing plan works at all levels. We can use it, as we have throughout the last few chapters, to put together a simple marketing strategy. We can also use the same model for individual examples of communications, or for briefing agencies, and we can use it to help define our brand.

If you're starting in business, or looking to get serious with your marketing for the first time, and don't have an established brand as such, then I hope working through the Offer–Goal–Activity model has given you not only a marketing strategy but also all the building blocks of a brand. If you're an established business and you already have a brand based on your existing offer and goals, you can refine your brand now you've worked through the Offer–Goal–Activity model.

I said earlier that a brand is much more than a logo, colour scheme and fonts. It's a combination of your offer, what people think of your products and services, and the experience they have doing business with you. Here's how you can use the model to either work on your brand from scratch or refine your existing brand. You can use what follows to brief a brand or design agency to help develop your brand image.

## Vision and mission

You derive this from your offer by describing where you want to be and what you want the work to look like at a set date in the future.

## Offer

You've answered these four questions:

— Who is your customer?

- What is their problem?
- How do you solve it better and different to anyone else?
- What's the minimum you can charge for it?

This has given you your product or service. It's what you do. It's your super-power, and it's what you want to be known for. What your customers say about your products and services defines your brand in their eyes.

## Goal

Again, you might link your brand goal to your offer, as described in your vision and mission. Your brand goal could be to succeed in your mission by delivering your vision.

## Activity

For your communications activity in your main Offer–Goal–Activity plan, you're talking about communications, advertising and promotions. For your brand, the activity you want to consider includes:

- values
- tone of voice
- logo
- colour scheme
- fonts
- imagery

Let's have a quick look at each of these.

## Values

We could argue that values could form part of the offer. Companies often brainstorm a whole series of words and phrases to describe themselves and what they do, and it's a valuable exercise to go through.

Beware, however, of simply coming up with words that describe what should be obvious values of all companies. I've seen financial advisers describe their values as being professional, friendly and approachable. Shouldn't all businesses be professional, friendly and approachable?

Remember, you're trying to be better and different to your competitors. What values do you have that set you apart from everyone else? It's also worth thinking about how your values relate to your people as well as your customers.

I think American Express's 'Blue Box Shared Values' is a good example of this.

*Customer Commitment:* We develop relationships that make a positive difference in our customers' lives.

*Quality:* We provide outstanding products and unsurpassed service that, together, deliver premium value to our customers.

*Integrity:* We uphold the highest standards of integrity in all of our actions.

*Teamwork:* We work together, across boundaries, to meet the needs of our customers and to help our company win.

*Respect for People:* We value our people, encourage their development and reward their performance.

*Good Citizenship:* We are good citizens in the communities in which we live and work.

*A Will to Win:* We exhibit a strong will to win in the marketplace and in every aspect of our business.

*Personal Accountability:* We are personally accountable for delivering on our commitments.

Back in 2001, I was part of a team of people who started a new financial services brand called Bright Grey. We put together a similar set of values, although we called them Drivers. We gave each member of staff a credit card-sized Driver Booklet that set out those values and we reinforced how important those values were at our regular daily team meetings and weekly company get-togethers.

## Tone of voice

This sounds like jargon, but it just means how you talk as a business. You've developed your offer so you know who your customers are and, therefore, you should know how they like people to talk to them. Hopefully, it's going to be in a simple, chatty, conversational way that engages them.

## Logo, colour scheme, fonts and imagery

To most people the combination of logo, colour scheme, fonts and imagery is what they would say is a brand but, having worked through the Offer–Goal–Activity model, we know it's much more than that.

If you're starting a business from scratch, my advice is not to dive straight in spending time and money on a logo, colour scheme, fonts and imagery. Perhaps come up with a temporary solution until you've nailed your offer and built your business. Then work on your visuals when it can be a true representation of your offer and your values.

Your offer, including the experience people have with your products and services, is what will shape what people think of your business.

As I said earlier, brand is a massive subject. But we can still use the Offer–Goal–Activity model to keep it simple. Give a good brand or design agency all the information set out in this chapter and they'll be able to help you come up with a great brand image for your business that reflects your offer and values.

# Offer–Goal–Activity marketing plan done

Congratulations. You've done it!

You've put together your Offer–Goal–Activity marketing plan and identified your strategy and tactics without the complexity often associated with academic or corporate processes. But there's one more important thing we need to do – perhaps the most important part of the process if we want to engage rather than enrage our customers.

As we start to put together our offer and activity, including developing products and services, drafting copy for content and adverts, and preparing outlines and scripts for audio and videos, we owe it to our customers to keep everything simple. This is particularly important in our communications.

In the last section of the book, we'll look at how we can keep everything simple.

But first here's a summary of all the sections of the Offer-Goal-Activity model.

# Offer–Goal–Activity marketing plan

| | |
|---|---|
| **offer** | Who is your customer? <br><br> What is their problem? <br><br> How do you solve their problem better and different to anyone else? <br><br> What's the minimum price you must charge to make a profit? <br><br> What's your one-liner? <br><br>    — Benefit 1 <br><br>    — Benefit 2 <br><br>    — Benefit 3 <br><br>    — |
| **goal** | What is the goal? <br><br> Why is the goal specific? <br><br> What is the plan to achieve the goal? <br><br> Why is the goal exciting? <br><br> Who'll hold you accountable? |
| **activity** | Content <br><br> Content advertising <br><br> Product/service/brand advertising <br><br> Price promotions <br><br> PR |

# Part five: Keeping marketing simple

# The rules of simplicity

Now we have our Offer–Goal–Activity marketing plan, as we put pen to paper – or fingers to keyboards – writing blogs or video scripts, adverts or newsletters, webinar outlines or podcast episodes, let's try and stick to the three rules for keeping marketing communications simple. These are:

- assume your customer knows nothing
- talk in your customer's language
- don't use jargon, management-speak mumbo jumbo or gobbledegook

## Assume your customer knows nothing

Earlier I talked about how marketers often project themselves and their own desires into their ideal customers. Marketers also suffer from something called the *curse of knowledge*. It's a bit of industry jargon, but because we live and breathe our products and services 24 hours a day, we understand the technicalities. We understand the jargon. And we understand the language surrounding our products and services because we immerse ourselves in it.

We often assume, mistakenly, that our customers understand it as well. But if we go piling in with our communications to customers using bloated language and complexity that *we're* immune to, it's an easy way to alienate them. It doesn't engage them, and if they're not engaged, they're less likely to want to do business with us. So, we've got to be aware of the curse of knowledge.

The best example I can give is from when I recently took my car for a service. I arrived at reception, handed over the keys and signed the paperwork. They then asked for my telephone number, so they could phone me if anything needed fixing. As always when I get my car serviced, I decided to go for a long walk because it usually takes a couple of hours. I walked along to Fisherrow Harbour to get myself a coffee.

After about an hour my mobile phone rang; the engineer from the garage wanted to talk to me about an issue with my car. He started talking in car technobabble. Petrolhead speak. All I heard was *blah blah, carburettor, blah blah, suspension, blah blah, petrol.*

I had to say to the guy, "Look, just slow down. I really haven't a clue what you're talking about. I don't speak car." And then he turned it round and just said it again in simple language, something like, "This is busted and if it doesn't get fixed, you might crash." Now I understood, and I was happy to give him the go-ahead to fix what needed fixing.

If you assume your clients know what you're talking about, very often you could alienate them. Like the car mechanic nearly did with me.

There's a difference between the complex knowledge of car maintenance and general knowledge you'd think everyone would have. I was watching the revamped 20th-anniversary shows of *Who Wants to be a Millionaire.* It's a quiz show that was incredibly popular when it first debuted two decades ago. Chris Tarrant hosted the show in its first run, but for the revamped version they brought in Jeremy Clarkson, ex-Top Gear presenter and now star of Amazon's *Grand Tour,* as the new host.

Watching the show and seeing how one of the contestants struggled with a question I thought was dead easy embodies why we need to assume our customers know nothing.

I can't remember exactly what question number it was, but it was high up the table. The lady was probably on about £8,000 or £16,000, around that. She'd used a couple of lifelines already and the question Jeremy Clarkson asked her was, "The Balearic Islands are a province of which country?" He gave her the four potential answers: France, Italy, Spain and Greece.

And I was sitting there thinking, well, it's bloody obvious, isn't it?

It's Spain.

We all know Mallorca, Menorca, Ibiza, Formentera are the Balearic Islands, don't we? Surely every single person in the UK and beyond has been to one of them? Think of all those people who go to Ibiza for the clubbing. All those people who go to Magaluf on stag and hen weekends. Everybody knows those islands, the Balearic Islands, are a part of Spain.

But this lady looked confused. She didn't know the answer. Jeremy Clarkson probed her a bit and asked if she wanted to use a lifeline. She decided to go for 50/50. Clarkson said, "Computer, take away two wrong answers and leave us with the correct answer and the one remaining wrong answer." The screen flashed and, after the musical sting, it left her with Italy and Spain. By now I'm on the edge of my seat screaming, "It's Spain! It's Spain! How can you not know it's Spain?"

The lady still wasn't sure. She stroked her chin and shared her thoughts out loud. She told Jeremy Clarkson she was convinced it was Italy. I was on my feet now. If the TV had a scruff of the neck, I'd have grabbed it.

Clarkson was calm in his role as the host. He didn't give anything away and kept a deadpan face. I sat back down, still agitated, as the lady talked herself into answering, "Italy."

"Final answer?" said Clarkson, still not showing any emotion. Now my wife joined in with my frustration. "No. No, it's Spain. How can you not know it's Spain? Mallorca! You must've been! Or to Menorca."

The lady confirms, "Italy. Final answer." Clarkson milked the atmosphere and tension. Paused, looking intently at the contestant.

Then, with despair in his voice, he said, "Oh! You've just lost £15,000." The collective groan from the audience echoed Clarkson's disappointment. The lady shrugged her shoulders and smiled. She was probably happy to go home with her £1,000.

The question she faced was one I thought everyone in the UK would have known the answer to. But she quite clearly didn't, and it cost her financially by derailing her journey to the million-pound question.

I started thinking about it from a marketing point of view. If you were a travel agent and you were putting together content for your website, you'd think about all the questions your customers might ask you about destinations, flights and hotels.

You probably wouldn't for a minute think anybody wouldn't know where Mallorca, Menorca, Ibiza and Formentera are. You probably wouldn't include something on your website pointing out Menorca is a Balearic island and is part of Spain. You'd probably succumb to the curse of knowledge of your own industry and assume everybody knows where those islands are. And you'd assume everybody knows which country those islands are a part of. But as *Who Wants to be a Millionaire* proved, there are people out there who don't know the answer.

It's why the starting point must be to assume your customer knows nothing. Once you assume they have a certain level of knowledge, there will always be people out there you'll exclude as a result.

Now, obviously, the Balearic Islands example is extremely simple. But what if it was a real technicality, like when I had my car serviced? Assuming a certain level of knowledge can confuse your customer. Okay, you might upset some people because they think it's just too simple and you're teaching granny to suck eggs but, personally, I think it's worth assuming your client knows nothing and just be relaxed that a few people might get upset by the basic level of information you're providing. The vast majority will love you for keeping it simple and, therefore, keeping it engaging.

So, rule number one, thanks to Jeremy Clarkson and *Who Wants to be a Millionaire*: assume the client knows nothing.

## Talk in your customer's language

Marketers often use bloated, complicated and officious language in their content and promotions. It's not how real people talk and, therefore, over-complex communications put customers off. They may not reach your call to action because they tuned out long ago.

Think about how you talk to your friends and family. Think about the last time you met a friend in the pub or in a cafe. Think about the language you use when you greet them, the language you use when ordering a drink, the language you use when talking about what you've been doing over the weekend.

It's chatty, informal. You don't use big words or passive language. And you don't use long bloated sentences that make you gasp for air through lack of punctuation.

If you were in the pub you'd say, "I'll get us a couple of pints of beer!" You wouldn't say, "Two pints of fermented hops in liquid form in a cylindrical transparent glass container manufactured from fused silicon will be procured for us at the bar by me." Imagine the look of horror that would creep across your friend's face if you used such language in the pub.

Even if you were meeting a business colleague in a coffee shop or bar, you wouldn't use overly formal language. You wouldn't use bloated words and sentences. You'd say, "Please take a seat." You wouldn't say, "Procure yourself a chair and lower your posterior carefully onto the seat by bending your knees until you feel your buttocks connect with the fabric." Imagine again the reaction on your colleague's face if you used such language!

If you wouldn't use such language when talking to friends, family and colleagues, why would you use it in your marketing communications? Perhaps as we grow up, attend school and go to college, institutions condition us to consider the written word to be much more formal than the spoken word.

When my son was going through school, he wasn't keen on English as a subject. He would often ask me for help with his homework. I'd look at his writing, and at once my eyes widened at the size of his paragraphs and the length of his sentences. I'd balk at his use of passive language.

He wanted help with the comprehension exercises, but as a marketing person my first instinct was to edit his text to reduce the length of his sentences and paragraphs. My marketing mind would want to rewrite his passive sentences in the active voice. But my son resisted this editing and insisted this was the way the school taught them to write.

Indeed, he was convinced he would lose marks if we edited his writing in the way I proposed. Long sentences get more marks, and massive paragraphs lead to higher grades. And, of course, at school they teach you to never start a sentence with the word *and*, and to avoid committing a load of other grammatical sins. Schools taught my son – and every other student in the UK – the written word should be bloated and passive.

A few years ago, we moved to a new house. It was the first time we'd moved in 18 years, and as you'd expect we took the opportunity to clear out some of the clutter we'd accumulated over the intervening years.

I was going through the boxes in the attic and the drawers in the wardrobes looking for things we could throw out when I came across a large red box file. For a moment I couldn't remember what was inside and, curiously, I opened the lid of the file. Inside were some old university scripts I'd written over 30 years before. The discovery surprised and delighted me, and I started to read.

The next thing I knew my wife was calling me and I realised a couple of hours had passed as I read through my old scribblings. What shocked me the most, after a marketing career of over 20 years, was the language I'd used in those university essays.

Looking down at the paper, I could see and recognise my own handwriting. Yes, these were handwritten scripts. I was at university long before word processors became accessible to the masses. My scrawl hasn't changed much in 30 years. Still plenty of loops and swirls and exaggerated 'S's.

But the language wasn't me. Most of it was passive and, like my son's essays, had incredibly long sentences with paragraphs taking up most of the page. It was full of big, important-sounding words and there was more than a hint of pomposity. I found myself laughing at the language I'd used all those years ago.

It reinforced my view that our educational system creates the impression the written word needs to be a whole lot more formal than the spoken word. It's why I believe marketing communications people allow bloat and complexity to seep into their marketing copy.

Add to this the belief in many corporates that longer words and passive language are somehow more professional, and you create an environment where we don't communicate in the language of our customers.

Here's another example. In another marketing role earlier in my career we'd put together an important client communication and I decided to put it out to a research focus group to make sure clients found it engaging and understandable. I sat behind a one-way mirror and watched the group discussing the content.

The people in the research group didn't like the brochure because they didn't understand it. They said the wording was full of dull corporate language and jargon, and they didn't feel like it talked to them. They said it wouldn't encourage them to take the action we wanted them to take, and it certainly wouldn't encourage them to buy stuff from us.

Armed with the research feedback, I went to my boss and told him we needed to start from scratch. He agreed I should go away and rewrite the brochure in plain, chatty English. We even got the Plain English Society to help us.

The second version was much better because I'd written it in the language of our customers. But guess what happened? When the legal and compliance people got their hands on it to sign it off, they rejected it. They said it didn't feel 'professional' enough. I argued, as I often had to, that if it wasn't breaking any rules and was legally sound they shouldn't reject it. But they dug their heels in.

And worse, they referred it to the executive team. Can you believe the piece of marketing material found its way onto the boardroom agenda?

The executive team told my boss to tell me to go with the original version of the brochure. The version people in the research groups had rejected. The version people said wouldn't encourage them to take the action we wanted them to take or to buy our stuff. The executive team agreed to let us put out a useless piece of literature just because it sounded more professional to them.

The more engaging brochure ended up in the bin.

One of the most effective ways of avoiding complexity and bloat is to write like you talk. Try using some dictation software on your computer or, better still, use the dictation facility available in most mobile phones. Phones are remarkably accurate and even allow you to speak the punctuation. Say "full stop" and one appears on screen, as if by magic. I completed the first draft of this book by using the dictation facility on my iPhone. You'll have to do a little bit of editing but, overall, it works a treat.

If you write like you talk then you've already made a massive leap ahead of many marketing communicators stuck in the complexity and bloat trap. Don't try too hard though. Some companies end up trying to sound too 'hip' and 'cool' to talk in their customers' language and it can misfire on them.

On a recent holiday, I found myself hating the in-flight announcements on the charter airline we were travelling with. It was all, "Ladies and gentlemen, boys and girls, we have an awesome flight lined up for you..." and "Wakey wakey, guys. We just wanna talk to you about some amazing in-flight duty-free offers."

The whole thing was grating, and I even found myself longing for the dull professionalism of British Airways. Maybe the charter airline just tried too hard to talk in the language of their customers, or maybe I'm not their target customer.

We need to strike a fine balance. Trying too hard to talk in the language of your customers, so it winds them up or annoys them, will be just as damaging as complex, bloated and passive language.

# Don't use jargon, management-speak mumbo jumbo and gobbledegook

Talking in our customer's language is hard when you work in an industry with its own jargon. But it's worth the effort to root it out and communicate in plain, simple and understandable language.

As well as industry jargon, another scourge blighting communication is management-speak. I mentioned earlier in the book that I'd asked for examples of cringeworthy management-speak in a post on LinkedIn. Here are some more, which I implore you to laugh at or joke about in the pub – but never, ever use in your marketing or any other communications.

**Going forward** is one of my pet hates. People don't need to say it. If you're going to do something, you can only do it from now into the future.

My favourite was ***deep dive***, and one MD used to mime the action every time they said it.

I'm guilty of saying *deep dive*. Though at least I don't do the arm movements. I also say *deep dive* when teaching people how to move into a forward fold in my yoga classes – but I think that's okay! Here's one of my favourites.

What about **actionable tips**? Isn't a tip by its very nature something you can act on? Are there such things as unactionable tips?

Then there's this gem.

**Growth hacker**. Sounds like you're hacking up a growth. Just sounds gross.

*Growth hacking* is horrible. I'm not keen on people using the word *hack* instead of tips, as in *15 hacks to keep the kitchen clean*. In the UK, Hacks are cough sweets.

And here's an extensive list of mumbo jumbo classics that deserve to be pinned on a dart board, not used in our communications.

- Circle back (usually said after they've 'reached out')
- Leverage

- Move up the value chain
- Let's take this offline
- Let's touch base
- Put a record on and see who dances
- Anything that begins with *agile*
- Let's punch a puppy (not literally – but doing something awful in business)
- Joined-up thinking
- From the get-go
- How can we get this onto his radar?
- Let's have a thought shower
- Look under the bonnet
- Let's peel an onion
- We'd better not let the grass grow too long on this one
- Let's park that idea for now
- Are you on all fours with that?
- How long is your runway?
- Let's lunch al desko
- Blamestorming!
- Let's kick the can down the road

And finally, one gentleman summed it all up like this.

The bigger the organisation, the more words are added into sentences that make no sense. My mum used to have a matrix of these words when she was at social services; it was called **bullshit bingo**. So, when someone inexplicably shouts out "Bingo!" during your presentation, you know your journey is at an end!

Okay, I'll put my hands up. I've used such language, even when I've been trying hard not to. But we really must stop it.

And what about clichés? If they say something is *unique* you know it is just the same as everything else. If it is *very unique* you know the copywriter doesn't realise you can't have degrees of uniqueness.

*Innovative* is equally meaningless, *game-changing* even more so.

Please don't tell me about *value added* or how something has been *optimised* so it reaches the *scalability* to become *world class*.

People want you to talk to them in plain English. It's how they communicate, both verbally and in writing. Here's another example of management-speak. It seems no noun is immune from someone turning it into a verb. *Let's cold towel the project.* As in, let's stop doing the project. A towel is a noun, obviously. But here they've used it as a verb.

Sadly, when it comes to management-speak mumbo jumbo, jargon and bloat, there doesn't seem to be any noun immune from being verbed.

And my final plea. Please don't use passive language in communications. Which of these sentences reads better to you?

*A letter full of marketing gobbledegook was sent to me by the marketing agency.*

or

*The marketing agency sent me a letter full of marketing gobbledegook.*

The first sentence uses the passive voice and the second the active voice. Businesses, especially big corporates, love passive language. With the active voice, the subject–verb relationship is straightforward. The subject does the work and the verb moves the sentence along.

With the passive voice, the subject of the sentence doesn't do anything. Some other agent or unnamed power does the work. The result is weak writing.

Perhaps it's why corporates like passive so much. It de-personalises the writing and masks responsibility; for example:

*Sorry, but your cheque wasn't processed on time by the accounts team.*

This is a passive sentence and it sounds like buck passing, doesn't it?

*Sorry, the accounts team didn't process your cheque on time.*

Much better. This is an active sentence, but it still hides responsibility.

*Sorry, we didn't process your cheque on time.*

Even better. An active sentence and taking responsibility.

Here's another example:

*Passive: There is a wealth of expertise shown by accountants when talking to their clients.*

*Active: Accountants show a wealth of expertise when talking to their clients.*

And another:

*Passive: The health and safety computer-based training must be completed each year by all members of staff.*

*Active: Each year, all members of staff must complete the health and safety computer-based training.*

You don't have to seek out and cut all passive language. But in business copy, where most writing is passive, someone who takes time to get active will stand out from the pack.

Active language is so much more engaging, but if you work in a big corporate, you'll find the passive is rife. Politicians also use passive language because it allows them to avoid taking responsibility. They'll say something like: "Mistakes were made during the design phase." Passive hides who made the mistakes. Wouldn't you have more respect for them if they just said, "We made mistakes during the design phase"?

There's an easy way to work out whether a sentence is passive or not. If you can add the words *by muppets* at the end and the sentence still makes sense, then it's passive.

*Mistakes were made during the design phase by muppets.*

If adding *by muppets* doesn't make sense, then you've cracked it —

the sentence is active.

*We made mistakes during the design phase by muppets.*

I urge you to do what I did when I worked in big corporate. Buy a gigantic red pen and use it to cross out passive language. Even better, you can use online language software like Grammarly to highlight it in red for you on screen. Then you can take great delight in hitting the delete key to obliterate passive language forever: wipe it out. Stay active and you'll be so much more engaging.

Those are the three rules for keeping your marketing communications simple. They apply equally to the written and the spoken words.

Here they are again.

— Assume your customer knows nothing
— Talk in your customer's language
— Don't use jargon, management-speak mumbo jumbo and gobbledegook

# Keeping it simple, from start-up to big corporate

## The cat mat rule

If you follow the three rules, you'll be able to keep your marketing messages simple and engaging across all mediums.

It's easier for small companies or start-ups to do this because they'll have fewer people involved in the sign-off process and everyone working for the company will understand the company's aims or vision. Indeed, it's likely they were involved in putting it together.

But as time goes by and the company grows, employing more people, it can become harder to hang onto the simple approach. Let's use an example. I use this in my conference presentations and the guests always give me great feedback. Not only is it a fitting example but it resonates with most people who hear it.

Let's pretend we work for a company making mats for pet cats. It's called *The Cat Mat Company.*

Imagine we're just starting work at *The Cat Mat Company.* On day one they ask us to attend an induction presentation. The CEO takes to the stage and talks about the company and what it does. She wants everyone to be able to say what the company stands for. A simple one-liner everyone can remember and learn instantly. The one-liner is a masterpiece of simple communication…

*Your cat sat on our mat.*

It's memorable, isn't it? Just by reading it you know what the company is all about.

Who are the company's customers? People with pet cats.

What does the company do? Makes mats for cats to sit on.

All the other stuff, such as why *The Cat Mat Company's* mats for cats are better than everyone else's, can come later. What's more, the one-liner is memorable and easy to learn.

In my presentation I show a slide to the audience for a few seconds and shout out the one-liner: "Your cat sat on our mat."

I then blank the screen and ask the audience if they could shout it out back to me. They usually shout, "Yes!" and so far, I've never failed to get the response I'm after. The audience shout out: "Your cat sat on our mat!"

I'm sure if you closed your eyes, you'd also be able to say this simple phrase back to yourself without having to check.

Whether delivered in the UK, the US, Europe or the Balkans, whether or not English is the audience's first language, they always respond.

But what happens when companies start to grow? It's not just the core people now, not just the originals who shared the start-up vision. What happens when a company grows and brings in people who weren't there at the start? Maybe it dilutes the vision? Maybe it creates internal division? Maybe it starts to add bureaucracy. More people might get involved in the sign-off process.

This is a dangerous time. This is when companies can start to lose control, complexity sets in, and they begin to fail on those three principles.

They start to assume their customers know more than they do. They'll convince themselves their customers will think badly of them for answering the 'bleeding obvious' questions. So, they won't anymore. But most customers still won't know the answers.

They start to talk in the language of their industry, not the language of their customers. It might only be the odd phrase, or it might be they start using passive language rather than active language because someone thinks it sounds more professional.

They start to use jargon, gobbledegook and management-speak mumbo jumbo.

They might get consultants in to verify their marketing strategy! They'll introduce complexity and start to use terms like SWOTs and PESTs and grids. They might start to lose sight of the important things, like engaging with customers.

Let's imagine now we're at the induction day for a bigger version of *The Cat Mat Company* to learn the one-liner.

*Our mat was sat on by your cat.*

The one-liner is still simple, and when I ask the audience to shout this one back to me, after counting them down *3 ... 2 ... 1 ...* they still get it right. But it sounds much more forced than the first one, more laboured. There's a moment of hesitation as they think about it more. It's because it's a passive sentence, not an active one.

Again, I'm sure if you closed your eyes, you'd also be able to say this simple phrase back to yourself, even though it's a little clunkier.

But as the company grows, and maybe adds more products, the one-liner starts to lose its simplicity. It's quite possible the consultants and their SWOTs and PESTs and grids make the company change their one-liner to something like this:

*Our mat was sat on by your cat, while playing with our innovative range of cat toys and eating our fishy munchies!*

It's still just about memorable, but it's lost its simplicity. The audience will give this a go, but after I've counted them in with *3 ... 2 ... 1 ...* they'll struggle. And this is usually the moment in the presentation where the penny drops, and they get the point of the example.

When they can't remember the one-liner to shout it back, they realise the effect complexity has on customer engagement. Could you close your eyes now and say the longer phrase back without checking?

If you work for a company and it's hard to remember its messages, if you can't repeat them back without reading them or checking them, what hope does the customer have?

The company continues to grow and now it's a big corporate. Now there are lots of different people from different organisations with diverse backgrounds. Maybe there's a leadership team who don't agree on goals and offers. Maybe they've developed silos and have a marketing department that doesn't talk to the sales team. Perhaps there's matrix management. It's a scary place when the marketing department is more like an agency you have to brief and where they don't work day in day out with you on the customer.

Staff might find they have conflicting SMART objectives and there might be more regulatory and compliance bureaucracy. It's become a place where they employ more people to count the beans than they do to grow the beans. And how do they get on with the three rules? They fail at them all.

They'll assume customers know all about what they do, and they'll stop answering the simple questions. Everyone knows the Balearic Islands belong to Spain, don't they?

Most of the language they use is industry language and they start to talk in this rather than the language of their customers.

Then there's overuse of jargon, gobbledegook and management-speak mumbo jumbo.

Strategy will be a long, painful process repeated annually and people will come to fear it. They'll spend millions on big international consultancies: PWC, Egremont, Tower's Watson. It becomes a massive intellectual exercise of SWOTs, PESTs, Boston Grids, Ansoff's Matrix, and Maslow's Hierarchy of bloody Needs! Strategic plans are hundreds of pages long and propositions become complex; the *why* of the company becomes confused and lost.

Let's imagine we're at the induction day learning the one-liner for 'big corporate'.

*The rectangular piece of coarse brown material, placed on the floor for people to wipe their feet on, was sat on by your small, furry, mottled ginger, grey and white feline creature with whiskers and pointy ears while playing with our innovative range of toys, developed using our own lean thinking and resilient, doctorate-level analytical research, and eating seafood manufactured from sustainable resources cooked to ISO2025 standards and meeting our environmental accountabilities.*

When I ask the audience to shout it back to me after a countdown, *3 ... 2 ... 1 ...* there is, of course, silence. And, most probably, knowing laughter. It's impossible, of course. No one can say it back without reading it out. Not even the leadership team. Simplicity is gone forever.

And there's probably one more problem with this one-liner! Can you guess what it is? The leadership team hasn't signed it off yet!

They're still arguing about the colour of the furry feline mammal (they need more detailed doctorate-level analytical research) and the legal team are concerned about the use of coarse material (Is it a danger to the customers and their cats?).

So, the leadership team are going to have an offsite awayday to refine the one-liner even more.

Now, of, course I've made some massive generalisations here. Some big corporates are massively successful and still manage to keep things simple, but many lose themselves in an abyss of complexity.

The 'Your cat sat on our mat' example works so well in a conference speech or a workshop. People laugh, they nod knowingly, they get it. It's a simple example of the dangers of complexity.

And while the example is about written communications, if you think about it, it's really a proxy for everything in business. Products can start out simple and then become blighted with complexity. Companies can introduce simple processes that become more bloated and annoying over time.

When you think about 'Your cat sat on our mat', don't just think about the marketing communications. Think about the product, the service and the processes.

What is your 'Your cat sat on our mat' product equivalent?

What is your 'Your cat sat on our mat' process or service equivalent?

Stick with it. Defend it from the ravages of complexity. Remember: simplicity engages, complexity enrages.

Which emotion do you want your customers to feel?

# Distance from the customer

Responsibility for keeping things simple, even when a company is growing fast, stays with the leaders, or with the original visionary who started the business.

It's hard. There will be distractions with the day-to-day running of a large company with many people and departments across multiple locations and teams with different disciplines.

But if the top team let complexity creep in, they'll find it almost impossible to stop it. If they don't set the tone, why would the rest of the company share a passion for simplicity? Indeed, if the top guys lose their passion for the values they held at start-up, and their people see them endorsing complexity, then everyone else will feel obliged to follow them along the same road.

Having worked my way up from a junior marketing assistant to marketing director and finally managing director, I've realised the more senior you get in a marketing role the further away from the customer you get.

Unless we consciously dedicate ourselves to keeping our customer focus, the other responsibilities and stresses of corporate life will conspire to throw us off track.

A marketing assistant might conduct some customer research confirming customers don't like that the company only offers its best prices to new customers. A customer-focused marketing assistant might feel uncomfortable knowing the company is happy to fleece existing customers with higher prices on the assumption they'll not go elsewhere.

But as a marketing director sitting at a board table, with the City of London watching your profit figures and share price and beating you up when they fall, you might be happy with higher prices for existing customers. You may see existing customers as cash cows. If you continue to fleece them, you'll make more profit.

Throughout my career, even at marketing director level, I forced myself to keep close to the customer. I'd still go out on the road and talk to clients. I'd attend research focus groups and listen in on customer service calls.

One day, one of the bosses from the group of companies I worked for called me into her office. The managing director of my business unit had recently resigned. As this was a financial services company, I fully expected the group boss was going to tell me they were bringing in one of the group accountants or actuaries to take on the managing director role.

She got to the point straight away. "We want you to take on the role of managing director."

We were in her office on the third floor and I'm sure my jaw dropped all the way through the floor and down through the two storeys below, crashing into the ground floor with a bump of disbelief.

"But I'm not an accountant or an actuary," I heard myself say.

"Exactly. You're a customer champion. And the company, indeed whole group, needs to be more customer-focused. You're definitely the man we want in the role."

I felt ecstatic, of course. Here was a massive opportunity – rather than being the lone customer voice on the leadership team, I could now set the tone.

But I failed.

Within six months in the role I realised I was further away from the customer than at any time in my career. Of course, I was now responsible for the whole company and not just the marketing team, and there were regulatory and corporate governance responsibilities as well. Not to mention a ton of corporate and group company committees with an insatiable appetite for time. And they had the power to overrule the managing director of the business units.

The crunch came when I had to disappoint, and ended up annoying, a load of important customers.

Every six months I'd put time in my diary to get out on the road with the sales team to meet customers. It might mean me doing a presentation, or simply visiting a financial advice firm to listen to what their advisors felt was going well and what they felt was lacking.

Everyone was busy and the sales team spent a stack of time setting up these sessions for me.

A couple of weeks before the road trip the group boss called me and queried why I'd blocked out my diary for a week. "Are you on holiday?" she asked.

I explained about the road trip. Her answer was to tell me – order me – to cancel the trip because the group was holding some governance and risk planning events. As my mind raced, I heard her mention risk exercises like running scenarios about what would happen to the company if a terrorist incident shut down the office. (Ironically, we never ran an exercise about what would happen if a virus pandemic shut down the world economy.)

I tried to argue how important the customer meetings were and even reminded her why she promoted me. She gave me no choice but to cancel.

Now, I know corporate governance is important when you get to the top level, as is risk planning. But the customer must be the most important focus. Having no customers is a risk no company wants to run. I had to phone the customers and the advisers and apologise for messing them about.

One said, "And you said you were going to be different. But you're just like the rest of the high-up financial types. You don't give a shit about the customer!" That comment hurt more than anything I'd heard in my career to date.

This episode hastened my departure from big corporate. When the company decided to go through one of its restructuring exercises, where everyone had to reapply for their jobs, I refused to take part. Even though they said I was likely to walk straight back in, I'd had enough.

Working with companies with a true customer focus was what I wanted to do. It was clear to me that, depending upon the culture and structure of a big corporate, even those in senior roles where the customer should be the focus are often deprived of their ability to serve the customer, because the voracious corporate appetite for short-term profits puts the customer second.

Even though a stronger focus on the customer might produce better profits over a longer period, it's usually the short-term financial results that companies prioritise. Only the most enlightened of leaders can make the change necessary.

As managing director of the business unit, I was the leader, and I tried to set the tone. But the group leaders didn't follow through on their promise. Maybe I should have fought harder. I often beat myself up about it.

But it's all in the past now. As an independent consultant and speaker, my focus is on the customer once more. And I'm enjoying working with businesses that feel the same.

# Part six: Summary

# The integrity of marketing

Congratulations. You now have all the tools you need to put together a simple marketing strategy focussed on your customers. Most importantly, you've designed the strategy to engage rather than enrage your customers.

Back at the start of this book, in some areas, I suggested marketing is broken

...unless it's done with integrity and a deep, almost obsessive understanding of the customer. There are many examples of companies and brands that lack integrity and an obsessive customer understanding, and I said it shows itself in three ways.

First, marketing just means communications.

We've solved this problem by thinking about research. By understanding customer needs and putting together an offer in the form of a simple product or service. By setting ourselves goals we can get excited about and have someone hold us accountable to. We did all this before starting to look at the communications.

The second problem I highlighted was marketing can be intrusive and annoying to the point it enrages the customer.

We've solved this by putting together engaging communications that don't intrude or annoy. By creating not just promotional material but content our customers might want to read or watch or listen to.

We can do this because our integrity and deep understanding of our customers tells us what kind of communications are acceptable and which cross the line.

I talked about the third problem with marketing: that products, services and communications are often complex.

We've solved this problem by fighting back against complexity: simple products, simple services and simple marketing communications.

I'm going to leave the last word to a fellow marketer, Allister Frost, who appeared on episode 203 of my *Marketing & Finance Podcast.* This quote sums up what it means to be good at marketing and embodies the integrity and understanding that I champion.

*Being a marketer is a huge privilege. Sometimes we lose sight of that because we get stuck in the day-to-day firefighting and problems and so on.*

*But it is an immense privilege to have an opportunity to communicate a message about a product or service to the right people to make their lives better and to improve their world.*

*And as such, we should view marketing and communications generally as an honourable, noble profession.*

*Sadly, it's one of the most disliked professions on earth because it's seen by some businesses as a cost and it's seen by the outside world as manipulation. They see us coercing people. Tricking people into buying stuff they don't need.*

*If you do marketing well, you should be able to look all of your family in the eye and say "This is what I do. I help connect the right solutions to the right people, so they can live their lives to the full."*

*We stop seeing it as a job just to sell, or to create leads, and we jump out of bed on a Monday and know it's all about customers. And we go and create something to help our customers and help people we understand to live their lives to the full, to buy the right things, to have the right services, to fulfil their dreams, to achieve their greatness.*

*That's when you suddenly realise, "Wow, this is a privilege."*

And it doesn't matter whether you're selling plumbing, cupcakes, coffee, courses or fitness clothing. It doesn't matter what you're doing. There are people who need to know what you've got because it will make their lives better. And if you do your job well, you'll connect those two things.

It must be for the betterment of society, and it must be for the betterment of the world. So, think of it as an honourable, noble profession and be proud of what you do. Have the highest standards of integrity and professionalism in all you do.

And you will create something that will stand the test of time and deliver some value to society as a whole.

# Appendix 1: Twitter search terms

*coffee shop*

Twitter will give you a list of tweets including the words *coffee* and *shop* in whatever order.

*"coffee shop"*

Twitter will give you a list of tweets including the exact phrase *coffee shop.*

*"coffee shop" near:UK*

Twitter will give you a list of tweets including the exact phrase *coffee shop,* in the UK.

*"coffee shop" near:Edinburgh*

Now Twitter will give you a list of tweets including the exact phrase *coffee shop* from the Edinburgh area.

*"coffee shop" or "pubs" near:Manchester*

This will give you tweets near Manchester that include the phrase *coffee shop* or *pub.*

*#CoffeeShop*

Tweets including the hashtag *#CoffeeShop.*

*"coffee shop" near:Edinburgh filter:links*

You'll get a list of tweets that include links. This could help your coffee shop research as it's likely the included links go to actual coffee shops' websites.

*"coffee shop" near:Edinburgh :)*

*"coffee shop" near:Edinburgh :(*

Adding either a smiley face or an unhappy face in the search term will give you a list of tweets that are all positive on the subject, or all negative on the subject.

Not only can you find out good and bad things about the subject you're searching for, but this is a good way to listen to what people are saying about your competitors. These are invaluable insights.

*"coffee shop" near:Edinburgh -breakfast*

You can be more specific again by asking Twitter to exclude certain phrases from your search. You might be interested in coffee shops, but not those serving breakfast. Use the minus sign before the phrase you want to exclude.

*"coffee shop" near:Edinburgh - "bacon roll"*

And remember the speech marks if you want to be more specific.

*"coffee shop"? near:Edinburgh*

Twitter will give you a list of tweets where people have used your search term in the form of a question.

# Appendix 2: Zombie storyboard

This is the script and the storyboards from the zombie video I talked about in the research section of the book. We decided the feedback was too polarised to go ahead with the production. What would you have done?

A standard, nondescript office. Barry, an attractive mid-30s office worker, is sitting with his feet up on the desk, a phone held in the crook of his neck, listening to a conference call. He's bored and looks over to one of his co-workers with a little bit of concern.

[General office noise]

Through the telephone we can hear a very boring nasal voice leading a conference call. "Okay, let's move onto point 3 of 56. A review of the southwest region's stationery sales."

Across from Barry we see his co-worker, Ed. A seemingly zombified co-worker, that is. The camera pushes in, and his head lolls forward.

Barry pulls a face. He doesn't think his friend looks in good shape. The HR assistant passes in front of Barry. Barry follows him with his eyes, aware of what is about to happen.

The conference call continues. "We had some rather exciting developments with our new page Post-it notes, very popular."

The HR assistant office walks uncomfortably behind Ed. As he speaks, Ed jerks his head up.

HR Assistant: "Ed, hi. Any chance we can have a word, in my

office?"

Ed groans in a very zombie-like manner.

The HR assistant strides past Barry, and Ed shuffles on. Barry covers the phone receiver and holds his hand out to Ed, grasping it in a firm handshake.

Barry: "Good luck, mate."

Unfortunately, Barry's strong grip ends up breaking off Ed's hand as he walks by.

[Ripping flesh noise]

Barry holds Ed's hand up and gags with exaggeration, trying not to let the conference call hear.

[Barry makes a controlled comic gagging sound]

Barry drops the hand into the wastepaper basket.

[Rustling of paper]

Ed shuffles into the HR office, and then collapses into the chair. He moves very much like a zombie would.

[Small groans with each step]

Barry cranes his neck to see into the meeting room. He moves the phone away from his ear so he can hear what is being said.

[Creaking of the chair]

The HR assistant sits down next to a fierce-looking female senior manager. "Listen, Ed, we've always loved your work. It's just some of your colleagues… They've started to complain. About the smell."

Manager: "To be frank, your standards have kind of slipped since you, err, died."

As much as a zombie can, Ed looks disappointed. He lifts his hands up to bury his face in them but stops as he notices and examines his missing hand.

Heartbroken, Barry looks for his friend; he then looks down at the picture of his own wife and son on his desk.

[Ed's groans from the office continue]

The HR assistant looks embarrassed and apologetic: it's as if Ed's groans had meaning. The manager is getting tired of this, however.

Manager: "Yes, we know you have a wife and daughter, but I'm afraid that really was – is – your problem, and we are going to have to let you go."

Ed slumps forward in the chair.
   [Groans]

Seen as a montage of quick shots: Barry presses disconnect on his conference call. He types something on his keyboard that we can't see. He runs his fingers along the search results (screen is bleached out by light so we can't make out which listing he has found).

[More groaning, but this time more agitated]

Looking back into the room with concern, Barry then quickly dials a new number he's seen on the screen.

The HR assistant leans in to whisper in the manager's ear.

HR assistant: "Oh, urm, well, maybe we could find a place for him in the call centre?"

The phone connects and Barry start speaking into the phone, getting increasingly concerned about the situation in the meeting room.

Barry: "Hi there, I'd like to talk to someone about getting some life insurance, to, you know, look after my family if I die."

In the meeting room, Ed half launches, half collapses over the table towards the senior manager. The HR assistant leaps back, petrified.

[Ed groans extra loud; the HR assistant makes panicky squeals]

Barry knows he must act. He speaks into the phone, then places it down on the table. The screen fades to white.

Barry: "I'm sorry, could you excuse me, just one second."

[Insurance Company logo comes up on the screen.]

"There are enough things to worry about if you die."

[Insurance company website URL comes up on screen.]

"Life insurance brought to you by Insurance Company – look after your family today and tomorrow."

The screen fades back from white. Barry and Ed are walking and shuffling down the hallway. Barry has one arm around Ed's shoulder, offering comfort. In the background, we see the senior manager and HR assistant peeking around the corner, watching them go.

Barry: "Listen, mate, why don't you and the family come over for dinner tonight, take your mind off things? Alison will make something nice."

Ed: "Brains?"

Barry: "Um, well, probably steak."

Printed in Great Britain
by Amazon